MITCHAM HIS



# MITCHAM BRIDGE, THE WATERMEADS AND THE WANDLE MILLS

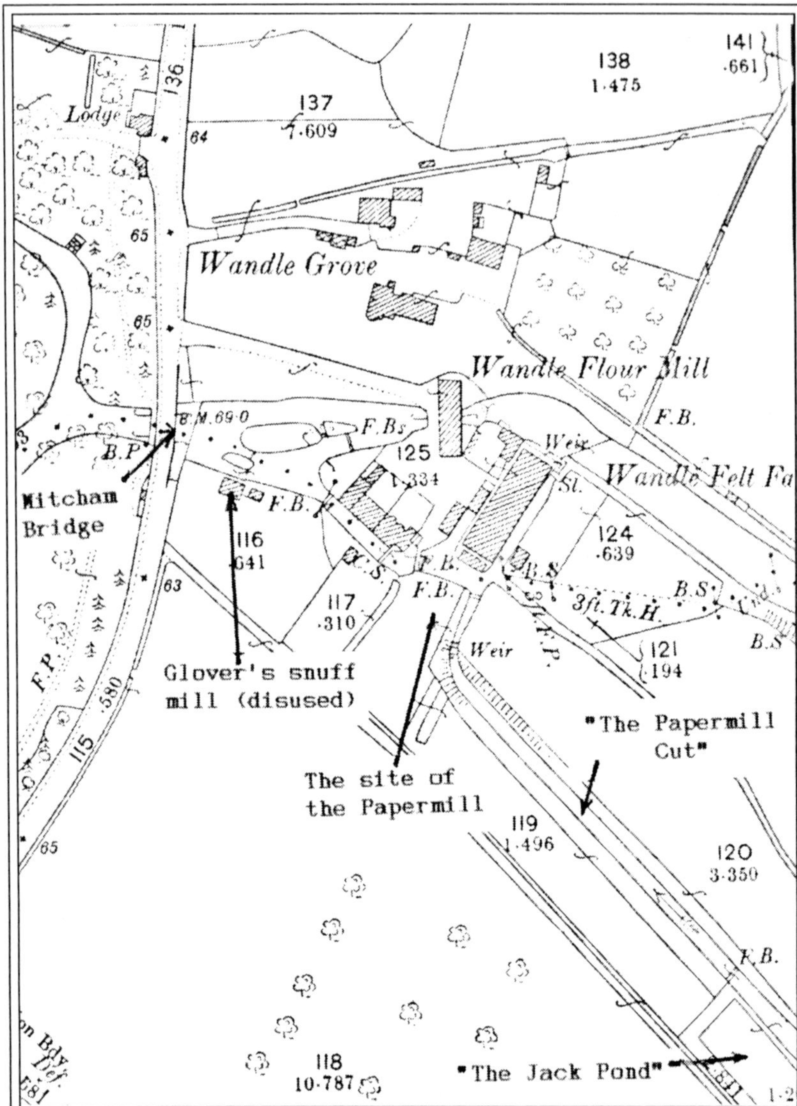


*Annotated extract from 25-inch Ordnance Survey map of 1894*

MITCHAM HISTORIES: 6

# MITCHAM BRIDGE, THE WATERMEADS AND THE WANDLE MILLS

E N MONTAGUE

MERTON HISTORICAL SOCIETY

Published by
MERTON HISTORICAL SOCIETY
2005



ISBN 1 903899 50 8

Printed by intypelibra,
Units 3/4, Elm Grove Industrial Estate, Elm Grove,
Wimbledon, SW19 4HE

***Cover Illustration:*** *Mitcham Bridge from Glover's Snuff Mill (print c.1800) reproduced courtesy of J A Goodman*

# INTRODUCTION

The Wandle, probably already in use as a convenient territorial boundary before the Roman period, was crossed by a ford from which, by the Norman Conquest, Lower Mitcham had derived its alternative name of Wicford.

It was here, long before the Domesday survey was conducted in 1086, that a watermill had been built - on a site which, over the next 1,000 years, saw many mills come and go. Until the advent of steam power presaged the demise of the humble watermill, this was the industrial heart of Mitcham, its output ranging from flour and copper goods, through paper and snuff, to felt and upholstery fillings. Even now, one mill building survives, until recently occupied by a firm specialising in chiropody products. Planning consent was obtained in 2003 for converting the building into flats, and the development of the land to the rear for residential purposes.

Remarkably, for it might well have evolved into a factory estate, the vicinity of the mill remained one of the most picturesque in the whole of Mitcham. In no small measure this is attributable to the Wandle itself, for since the Middle Ages the river's banks provided sites for several large houses, the grounds of which were to survive, substantially intact, until the social upheavals of the early 20th century.

The need to preserve open spaces for public enjoyment was recognised by the mid-19th century, but it was the growing momentum of urbanisation, apparent even in Mitcham before the end of the Victorian era, that added urgency to efforts to save for posterity what remained of the rural Wandle. Largely inspired by the enthusiasm of Octavia Hill, one of the three co-founders of the National Trust, the River Wandle Open Spaces Committee came into being, and it was through their efforts that the Watermeads passed into the care of the Trust shortly before the outbreak of war in 1914.

Since then, the surrounding area has changed almost beyond recognition. With one exception the prestige houses of the past have gone, but miraculously substantial portions of their grounds abutting the river escaped redevelopment and remain as parkland to which the public have access. National Trust land and municipal parks alike are now linked by a new concept, the Wandle Trail, which provides pedestrian access to the riverside through what, happily, remains one of the most attractive corners of urban Surrey.

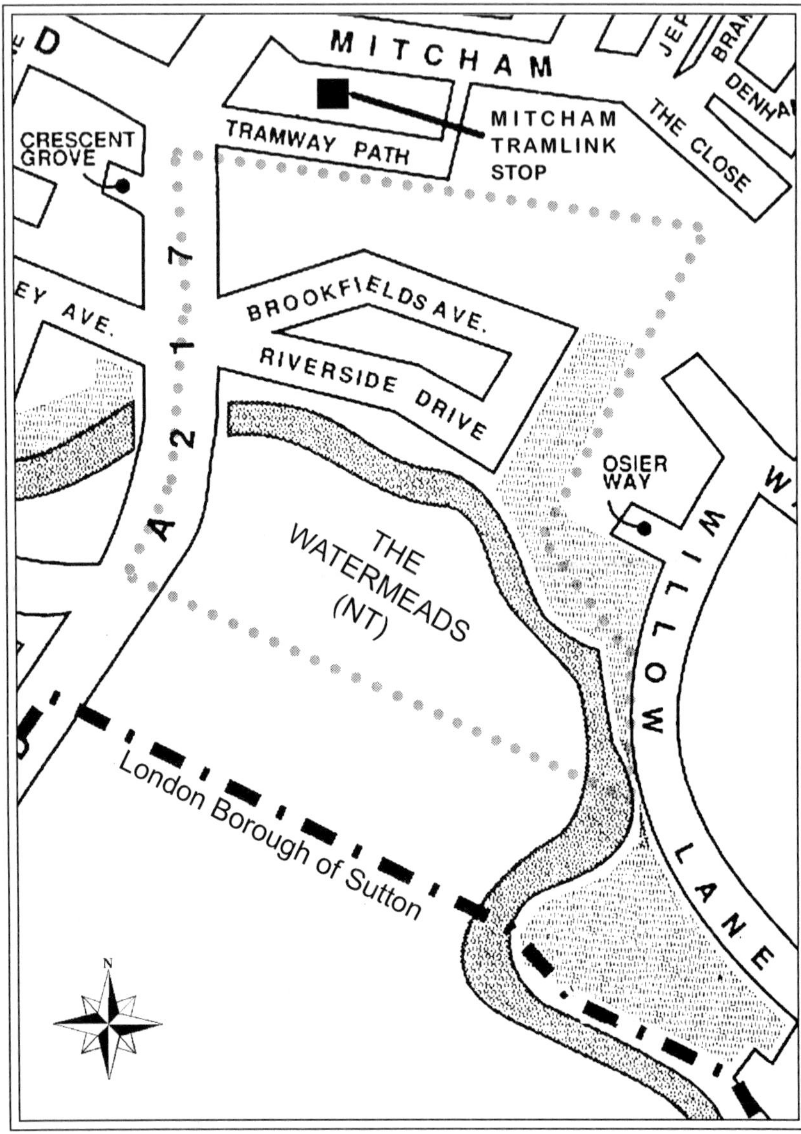


*Detail from a modern street map, showing the area covered by this book outlined with a dotted line. Reproduced by permission of Merton Design Unit, London Borough of Merton*

# CONTENTS

# MAPS AND ILLUSTRATIONS

# ACKNOWLEDGEMENTS

Material for this book was gathered over a period of almost 40 years in a quest which was both fascinating and challenging, and proved a pleasurable exercise with help and encouragement from numerous archivists and librarians. As always, staff of the Surrey Record Office and Merton Central Reference Library (my main sources) were particularly helpful – a tradition now followed in exemplary manner by their successors in the Surrey History Centre and Merton Local Studies Centre. To them I owe many thanks, and trust they will forgive my not mentioning them by name.

Finally, I would also like, once again, to express my sincere gratitude to the editorial subcommittee of Merton Historical Society, Judith Goodman, Peter Hopkins and Tony Scott, for their meticulous checking and tactful corrections of early drafts without which some embarrassing slips might well have become enshrined in print.

E N M

Sutton 2004


**Imperial Measures are used throughout this book**
**1 acre = 4 roods = 160 square rods, poles or perches = 0.4047 hectares**
**1 mile = 1.6093 km**
**1 yard = 3 feet = 0.9144 metres**
**1 ton = 2240 lb (pounds) = 1.016 tonnes**
**1 lb (pound) = 0.4536 kg**
**1 gallon = 4.546 litres**
**£1 = 20s (shillings) = 240d (pence)**

*Mitcham Bridge and the Wandle ford from the South.*
*Early 20th-century post card*

*View of Mitcham Bridge and the ford looking south*
*(Photograph c.1910 from the Tom Francis collection, reproduced by courtesy of Merton Library Service)*

# Chapter 1

## MITCHAM BRIDGE

From time immemorial, travellers on the high road south from Mitcham to Sutton have been obliged to cross the river Wandle, which here was used to define the ancient boundary between the parishes of Mitcham and Morden and, until 1965, the southern limits of the Borough of Mitcham. Long before either of the two communities could afford the luxury of a bridge the crossing would have been via a ford, which older residents can still remember as a watersplash at the side of Mitcham Bridge.

In the 13th century, and for much of the later Middle Ages, Lower Mitcham was known as Wicford or Wickford, a placename prompting speculation that it might be translated as the 'ford of the *vicus*', the latter being a word of Latin derivation commonly used to denote a settlement.[1] Traces of occupation during the Romano-British period have been found at several sites in Lower Mitcham, and the evidence of the large 'Dark Age' cemetery between the Wandle and Morden Road, which was in use for 150 years or so from about AD450, demonstrates that a not insignificant population continued in the area into the fifth and sixth centuries.[2] The ford remained visible at the side of the bridge until the 1940s, although no longer used by vehicles and wired off to deter access. As part of the measures to defend the bridge during the anti-invasion preparations of 1940 the roadway was narrowed with large concrete blocks, and the ford was rendered impassable to traffic by iron girders driven into the river bed, creating what were optimistically dubbed 'tank traps'. They had all been removed by 1945, and within a few years the roadway was widened and the bridge extended over the old ford to provide a footpath for pedestrians.

If the bridge is noticed at all today by the passing motorist, it is as a slightly inconvenient restriction in the otherwise wide road south of the former Mitcham station, (now the Tramlink stop). It might appear to be relatively modern, but a metal parish boundary plate fixed to the western parapet bears the date 1882 and shows that, at least in part, the structure is already well past its centenary.

Over 300 years ago, when James II was still on the throne, another Mitcham bridge spanned the Wandle at this point.[3] Expenditure on bridge maintenance, a burden on the highway rates, was commonly avoided by parochial authorities if at all possible, and in 1725, when repairs were necessary, Lt Gen Daniel Harvey, Governor of the State of Guernsey, who was resident at Mitcham Hall, Lower Mitcham, and presumably had influence in such matters, undertook to "use his best endeavours" to secure the cost did not fall on the parish of Mitcham.[4]

In 1759 the bridge again needed attention, and Mitcham and Morden were formally 'presented' to the magistrates of the county for neglecting to keep the bridge in a proper state of repair.[5] The procedure was a well-established one, and in default of the parishes it was customary for the works to be carried out by the county. Local records do not tell whether the bridge was of wood or more durable material, but by 1789 it was certainly of brick and the fact sufficiently impressed Edwards, the topographical writer, for him to comment on it in his *Companion from London to Brighthelmston.*[6] An early 19th-century engraving depicts the bridge as having three semi-circular arches (see cover), as does a watercolour by Hassell, dated 1823. These arches can be seen in photographs and postcards of a century later, and are still visible from Morden meadow today.

*Mitcham Bridge and the ford. Postcard c.1910*

# Chapter 2



## THE WANDLE FISHERY

For centuries the Wandle, fed by springs emerging from the chalk along the dip slope of the North Downs between Croydon and Carshalton, was a trout stream of deserved repute. Camden, writing in 1586, referred to the "clear little river Wandle, full of excellent trouts",[1] and early in the 17th century sport on the section between Merton and Wandsworth was so good that it was necessary to safeguard what was then regarded as a 'Royal Preserve'.

Thus in 1606 a Sampson Calvert was charged with the protection of the king's game below Merton Abbey, and there is record of the frequent granting of similar warrants throughout the century. Hobson, in his *Book of the Wandle*, tells how in 1623 Sir Edward Cecil, later Viscount Wimbledon, was given responsibility for the conservation of "river-fish" in the Wandle as far as Mitcham, his authority reinforced with the power to offer a 20 shillings reward for the apprehension of offenders. The warrant was renewed two years later. At least one poacher, Thomas Barker by name, is recorded as being caught and taken into custody for poaching fish between Croydon and Wandsworth in 1640, and one imagines that there were many others whose activities escaped detection.[2]

Between Mitcham and Beddington trout up to three pounds in weight were commonplace at the beginning of Victoria's reign, the Revd Herbert Randolph, for instance, when a curate at Mitcham, recording in his diary for May 1st 1838 that whilst fishing "at York's mill" (at the end of Willow Lane) he "caught 3lb., 2½lb. and 1½lb. trout".[3] Sir Humphrey Davy, according to whom the grannum, brown fly and the blue dun were the principal flies used at this time, fondly recalled delightful days angling "in the shady green meadows by the bright clear streams of the Wandle".[4] The author Cecil Torre, remembering his boyhood, also described the fishing on the Wandle in the mid-19th century:

> "From 1866 until his death in 1878 my father had some fishing on the Wandle a little way from Mitcham, which was then a quiet country village with fields of lavender and roses for making scented waters ..." Fish a pound or less "were thrown back in the Wandle to

> let them have a chance of growing bigger. There were trout of two or three pounds there, and a few such fish make a good catch. As a matter of fact, the catch depended much more on the landing-net than on the rod and fly. I had to take the landing-net, while my father played his fish; and that cured me of what little love I had for fishing."[5]

As late as the 1880s when, according to Tom Francis, there were some 20 varieties of fish to be found in the Wandle, it was not uncommon when looking over the parapet of Mitcham bridge to see trout lying on the bottom of the crystal clear stream, their speckled backs blending with the stony bed of the river.[6]

Although we are now only too well aware of its effects, pollution of our environment is nothing new, and as long ago as the 1860s a number of people, including local landowners and anglers, were seriously concerned at the deteriorating condition of the river. In January 1861 a paper by Frederick Braithwaite entitled 'The Rise and Fall of the River Wandle' was presented at a meeting of the Institution of Civil Engineers under the chairmanship of George Parker Bidder.[7] The reading of the paper was followed by a long and earnest discussion in which Sir John Rennie and other distinguished members took part. Bidder, himself an eminent civil engineer and president of the Institution, was then living at Mitcham Hall, and owned a large estate in Mitcham and Morden, either side of the Wandle below Mitcham bridge. Sharing his neighbours' fears that the river would soon become unable to support the excellent trout which still abounded in its upper reaches, he deplored the uncaring attitude of the proprietors of the tanneries and textile printing works who used the Wandle as a sewer, and daily allowed the discharge of large quantities of partially decomposed organic waste and harmful chemicals into the very river upon which they themselves were so dependent.

Paradoxically, one of the principal agents of pollution was the Croydon Local Board of Health which, whilst providing a main drainage system for the benefit of the rapidly growing town of Croydon, in the 1860s discharged into the Wandle effluent from its newly opened sewage farm at Beddington after only minimal treatment. Incensed at the death of fish in his section of the Wandle, Bidder took legal action against the Croydon authority in an effort to force the adoption of more effective measures to prevent the nuisance recurring. This had little lasting effect, and in 1877 the newly created Croydon Rural Sanitary Authority found itself facing censure for the poor quality of the effluent it was allowing to pass from its sewage farm at Beddington into the Wandle at Mill Green. Further proceedings, this time initiated by Bidder's son, a Queen's Counsel, resulted in a permanent injunction being granted, restraining the authority from polluting the river. Regrettably the improved sewage treatment measures which were functioning towards the end of the century proved too little and too late. The industrial effluents which Bidder senior had deprecated in the 1860s declined for reasons totally unconnected with any wish to save the fishing, but any trend towards improvement in the state of the river was soon nullified by the discharge of waste from the new factories gradually spreading throughout the upper Wandle Valley, as well as the steadily increasing volume of effluent from the sewage works.

Despite local agitation and the efforts of the authorities, the Wandle was therefore never to regain its pristine condition, although towards the turn of the century there seems to have been some confidence that the deterioration had at least been halted. At this time the exclusive fishing rights in the river from Willow Lane to Ravensbury Mill were owned by William F J Simpson of Park Place, Mitcham, Sir Frederick Ferrars Conant Fowke of Lowesley Hall in Leicestershire, and George Parker Bidder QC of Ravensbury Park, who became the owner of the family estate shortly before the death of his father in 1878. Together they decided to form the 'Wandle Fisheries Association', with the object of conserving fish stocks and improving the sport. By 1895, Henry Bourne, whom they appointed as their bailiff, had been installed in the weatherboarded Wandle Cottage, now No. 475 London Road,[8] and a trout hatchery was established in the security of the Watermeads.[9]

In 1906, for reasons which are not clear, the Wandle Fisheries were leased for five years to Croydon Corporation (the town achieved county borough status in 1889). Harry Bourne vacated what had by then become known as 'Fisheries Cottage' the following year[10] to become groundsman and umpire for Mitcham Cricket Club, and after ten years or so of careful husbandry his former charges were left to their fate. On termination of the lease disputes arose over the condition of the river, and in particular continuing pollution by effluent from Croydon's Beddington works. Eventually a settlement was reached, and in December 1912 the corporation agreed to pay William Simpson, Sir Frederick and Captain Harold Bidder (who had inherited part of the Ravensbury estate on the death of his father, George Parker Bidder II in 1896) damages totalling £1,500 over a period of 10 years, and further undertook to double the damages to the aggrieved parties if, after the expiration of the agreed period, the pollution had increased.[11]

Shortly after moving to 'Ravensbury Manor', the fine neo-Georgian house he had built for himself on the banks of the Wandle in 1912, Harold Bidder made a further attempt to restore trout to the Wandle, introducing young fish to the water running through what is now Ravensbury Park. Once again, the bid failed, this time, it was commonly believed, due to pollution of the river by surface water drainage from the newly tarred roads.[12] Although a few fish were to survive into the late 1920s, the dissolved oxygen levels were too low to support trout, and the efforts at restocking can now be seen as forlorn rearguard actions.

Bidder rejoined his regiment on the outbreak of war in 1914, and served with distinction, being awarded the DSO and rising to the rank of lieutenant-colonel.[13] He had left a village Mitcham in which squire and gentry still held sway, but returned to an urban district soon to be changed almost beyond recognition by its expansion into a London dormitory suburb. William Simpson, no longer interested in fishing, moved away from Mitcham before the Armistice,[14] and Ravensbury Manor was soon to be demolished to make way for new housing. A fraction of the Bidders' once extensive estate was purchased by the urban district council of Mitcham, acting jointly with that of Merton and Morden, and opened as a public park in 1930, but all hope of reviving the fisheries had obviously vanished.

By the 1930s depletion of the springs by heavy and widespread extraction of water from the chalk aquifer, increasing pollution from industry on the river banks upstream from the Watermeads, plus the effluent from the sewage disposal works at Beddington were, regrettably, combining to reduce the river to little more than an open sewer, and very little fish life survived.

The next four decades witnessed the final descent of the middle and lower reaches of the Wandle to a dark murkiness, devoid in many sections of all but the most tenacious forms of aquatic life. At Mill Green, where the still relatively unsullied water issuing from the springs between Croydon and Carshalton was joined by the effluent from the Beddington works a dramatic change in the condition of the river was obvious to the most casual observer. By the 1950s 90% of the normal dry weather flow in the river below Mill Green was, in fact, treated sewage. This was a period during which synthetic detergents were making their appearance and, the foaming agents being non-biodegradable, they passed through the treatment works without destruction. As a result, by the late 1960s the Wandle was often disfigured by masses of floating foam, the river at times completely disappearing from view beneath a blanket of froth several feet deep where the water was turbulent. The situation was particularly bad between Mitcham Bridge and a new automatic level control gate and weir installed by Surrey County Council in the Watermeads.

It was, however, an unprecedented discharge of partially digested sludge from the Beddington works in the summer of 1969 which brought about the temporary eclipse of the Wandle as an amenity, giving rise to a spate of complaints not only from the general public but also from the National Trust at the stench emitted by the evil-looking water. Merton health department reacted by recommending the termination of children's boating on a stretch of the river flowing through Ravensbury Park, and in the summer of 1970 a notice was erected by the Greater London Council warning of the danger of allowing children to paddle in the polluted water below the Beddington outfall, for which the authority was then responsible.

A new activated sludge treatment plant became operative at the works in 1970, but two years passed before some improvement became apparent in the Wandle. Scoured by the run-off from unseasonal rainstorms, the debris-strewn gravel of the river bed was then once more dimly visible through the cloudy water. There was also a steady decline in the foam, due to the co-operation of the manufacturers and the increasing use of 'soft' detergents, capable of being broken down by bacterial action in the filter beds. Gaily painted paddle boats again became available for hire in the park, albeit only temporarily, and a few sticklebacks miraculously reappeared to encourage the hope that the Wandle was perhaps on the way to recovery.

By the mid-1970s experimental restocking of the upper reaches of the river with trout by the Thames Water Authority, and the re-introduction of coarse fish to the lower reaches, conveyed the impression of official optimism that improved pollution control measures were becoming effective. In July 1973 it was demonstrated that trout were capable of surviving in the Wandle for several months, a few specimens in a cage having been immersed experimentally in the Watermeads downstream from the sewer outfall. Machines were brought in to clear the 'Jack Pond' of silt and weeds, and in May 1977 arrangements were made with the Mitcham Angling Club for its members to take over management of the pond under licence granted by the National Trust. Stocking was undertaken by the National Rivers Authority, and the pond soon contained a good variety of coarse fish including the three common species of carp, plus tench, roach, bream and perch.

Current management policy is directed towards maintaining the fishery, with judicious restocking, following routine silt removal and weed clearance. Given the improved state of the river, it is hoped that pollution will not present a serious problem, and the vigilance of the anglers, who have an obvious interest in excluding unwanted intruders, should prove a valuable reinforcement to the efforts of the Trust to protect the Watermeads from abuse and vandalism.

Accidental, rather than deliberate, discharge of oil and toxic wastes from the riverside factories via the surface water sewers, and heavy metals which remain in the effluent from the sewage treatment works, now present the major risk to wild life in and on the river itself. One such discharge, in September 1973, was of cyanide, accidentally released into the river by a Beddington firm, and resulted in the loss of a large proportion of the fish recently introduced into the main river. A year later a heavy discharge of diesel oil from a fractured pipe at the Central Electricity Generating Board's power station at Croydon killed fish and waterfowl downstream as far as Morden Hall Park. A further example of the river's vulnerability to pollution occurred more recently, when over a period of several days in October 1995 the discharge of a large volume of only partially treated sewage from the Beddington treatment works killed the entire fish stock, not only in the Jack Pond but also in virtually the whole of the Wandle downstream from Mill Green.[15] Continuing improvements by Thames Water at the Beddington works have enabled the ecology of the Wandle to recover, and by the turn of the century the water quality was declared 'good' by the Environment Agency. However, it would be naive to imagine accidents such as these will not recur.

With responsibility for management of the river today firmly in the hands of the Environment Agency, and an expressed commitment on the part of the London Boroughs concerned to ensure that the full amenity potential of the river is achieved and maintained, the layman can only trust that their joint efforts will succeed when in the past attempts have all too often failed.

*The Wandle upstream from the Watermeads. Postcard c.1905 (The site of the future Willow Lane industrial estate lies to the left, and what was to become Poulter Park is to the right.)*

*The former 'Fisheries Cottage', seen from Mitcham Bridge in 1967 (ENM)*

*'Paper Mill Cut' in the Watermeads c.1990 (ENM)*

# Chapter 3



## THE WATERMEADS AND HAPPY VALLEY

### Acquisition by the National Trust

The Watermeads and 'Happy Valley', lying either side of Mitcham Bridge on the A217 from Mitcham to Sutton, are part of the 139 acres of riverside land which comprise the National Trust's Wandle Properties, and are situated almost entirely within the London Borough of Merton.[1]

The original 12 acres forming the heart of the Watermeads are to be found upstream from the bridge, mainly on the south bank of the river but also including a small island and strip of woodland on the north bank adjoining the private roadway leading to the Grove Mill. This also gives access to three former mill cottages, numbered 475-479 (inclusive) London Road and the site of the Crown Mill. Planning consent for redevelopment of land behind the mills for housing purposes having been granted by the local authority, building work commenced in 2004.

The Watermeads have the interesting historical distinction of being amongst the first properties to be acquired by the Trust, and were purchased from Sir Frederick Fowke with £1,050 raised by the River Wandle Open Spaces Committee, completion of the conveyance taking place in November 1913.[2] It is said the appeal for funds, the last with which Octavia Hill, one of the Trust's founders, was to be involved, was largely inspired by her enthusiasm after having seen holiday makers on the river banks and children paddling at the water's edge.[3] Octavia Hill, who died in 1912, unfortunately did not live to witness the formal presentation of the Watermeads to the Trust by the committee the following year. Miranda, her sister and fellow worker in efforts to improve the housing of the poor, had died in May 1910, and a red stone seat donated by her pupils and inscribed to her memory can be seen overlooking the mill-cut in the Watermeads.[4]

The so-called 'Happy Valley', two acres on the south bank of the river downstream from the bridge had, like the Watermeads themselves, once formed part of the extensive Mitcham Grove estate owned by banker

Henry Hoare in the late 18th and early 19th centuries. The estate was bought by Sir John Lubbock, another banker, after Henry Hoare's death in 1828 and eventually Happy Valley was purchased from the Lubbock family in 1846, together with much of the adjoining land, by George Parker Bidder.[5] Following the death in 1896 of his son, George Parker Bidder QC, the dismembering commenced of what had become known as Ravensbury Park (embracing much of the land to the south of the river towards Rose Hill), and a substantial portion was divided up and offered for sale as building plots. The two acres lying alongside the river were donated to the Trust in 1915 in memory of Octavia Hill by Richardson Evans,[1] who in 1903 had founded the John Evelyn Club of Wimbledon - since 1982 the Wimbledon Society and still one of Merton's premier amenity societies.

Happy Valley is now part of a green corridor linking the Watermeads with Ravensbury Park and, although not accessible to the general public,[6] has an important role in preserving the attractiveness of this stretch of the river by screening from view the rear of houses in Wandle Road on the south bank. Since the outbreak of Dutch elm disease in the early-1970s, as a consequence of which many trees had to be felled, and the devastation caused by the great storm of October 1987, Happy Valley has lost some of its unkempt charm. Natural regeneration is, however, gradually making good the damage. Redevelopment by the London Borough of Merton of the former grounds of Mitcham Grove as a housing estate in the late 1970s altered dramatically the appearance of the north bank of this stretch of the river, but the creation of a lake (a flood alleviation measure), combined with replanting and landscaping and a new riverside path, has formed what is, in effect, a linear park following the river downstream from Mitcham bridge through Ravensbury Park to the Trust's Morden Hall estate.

The wrought-iron Gaston Gate, through which keyholders once gained access to Happy Valley from Bishopsford Road, is now used only for maintenance purposes. It commemorates Alderman S L Gaston, who was 'father' of Mitcham Corporation in the mid-1930s, and chairman of Mitcham Urban District Council when what remained of the grounds of Ravensbury Manor was formally opened to the public by George

Lansbury MP in 1930. Alderman Gaston became mayor of Mitcham in 1937, and for many years was chairman of the Mitcham Civic Society, actively lending his support to efforts at conserving and enhancing the surviving open land on the banks of the river.

An additional acre of land on the south bank of the river, known as Morden Meadow and lying between Bishopsford Road and the actual Watermeads, was donated to the Trust by the Urban District Council of Merton and Morden in 1965, following completion of flood control work by Surrey County Council. The meadow now forms an integral part of the Watermeads, to which it gives access, and is the first part of the property to be seen by visitors entering from the Bishopsford Road gate. At the water's edge one can find an edge-runner mill stone and see the brick revetments and sill in the river bed marking the position of Richard Glover's Morden snuff mill. This seems to have been built in about 1804. (Its history is dealt with on pages 43-5). The picturesque slate-roofed and weatherboarded building survived long after it had fallen into disuse, and the undershot wheel was not completely dismantled until the mill was demolished for safety reasons in 1922.[7]

*The site of Glover's snuff mill seen from Morden Meadow, May 1967 (ENM)*

## The Early History of the Watermeads

The origins and early history of what today are known as the Watermeads are obscure, but it seems that in the 13th and 14th centuries the waterside meadows formed part of the extensive estate in Mitcham, Morden and Carshalton of the de la Mare, or de Mara, family who then held the lordship of the manor of Ravensbury. In 1362 William "Mareys" (the spelling varies considerably) of Mitcham granted "his capital messuage with houses over, gardens, crofts, meadows, pastures, woods, trees, hedges, hays and ditches as enclosed, together with two water mills and a piece of moor [i.e. waste or marshland] adjoining as enclosed by the water towards Beneytesfeld and all appurtenances in Wykeford" at 100 shillings per annum to Sir Richard Porter, perpetual vicar of Mitcham and Sir John de Scaldewell, perpetual vicar of "Westmorden".[8] The site of William Mareys' house is unknown, but one landmark, 'Bennett's Hole' or 'Hollow', is still marked at a bend in the Wandle upstream from the Watermeads on OS maps. Beneytesfeld is thus identifiable with part of today's Poulter Park, and there is little doubt that some, if not all, of the land we now know as the Watermeads was included in William Mareys' gift to the Church. The precise nature and significance of this conveyance is not fully understood at the present time, but it may be more than a coincidence that the transfer occurred when the Black Death was at its peak. Not only was the economic base of the country at this time severely affected, but men's minds were increasingly preoccupied with their mortality, and the perceived need to make their peace with God. By the middle of the 16th century, following the Dissolution of the monasteries, ownership of the property was once more in lay hands.

It is to be assumed from the name and the location of the Watermeads that, together with other marshy land on the Mitcham side of the river, they would have been managed in the Middle Ages as an important resource, providing winter fodder and rich summer pasture. Every winter the land would have been flooded, either naturally or by the manipulation of sluices, the silt deposited by the river water enriching the soil. Each spring, once the water had drained off, the lush growth of fresh grass and herbage would be gathered for hay, after which the meadow would have been grazed by cattle, their dung adding further enrichment to the soil. Alternatively, the land could have been allowed to flood again, and a second fodder crop removed in late summer. What could be evidence of this regime can be seen in the artificial channels which still conduct water through the low-lying area between Paper Mill Cut and the main river.

## The Mill Sites

The Domesday survey of 1086 shows that even before the Norman Conquest the power of the Wandle had been harnessed to grind corn, and by the mid-19th century, when the general availability of steam power was weakening the bonds tying industry to the waterside, the river was used virtually to the limit of its potential. James Malcolm, in an often misquoted comment in his *Compendium of Modern Husbandry of Surrey*, published in 1805, speculated that "for its length and size, perhaps no river in the world does at this time furnish so many valuable and various manufactories ...".[9]

The sites of two watermills operating in the early 19th century can be found within the National Trust's Watermeads property. One, known as Morden Mill, was used for the grinding of snuff, and stood close to the bridge where, as we have remarked earlier, a millstone can be found beneath a tree on the river bank. The second was located further upstream, where a prominent feature confronting the visitor is the tumbling-bay and tailrace at the end of what is still known as 'Paper Mill Cut'. The site of the paper mill buildings, which disappeared well over a century and a half ago, is now the rectangular grass-covered plot separated from Morden Meadow by a hedge. The history of both mills will be dealt with in more detail later, together with an account of other mills on the opposite bank of the Wandle, in Mitcham parish.

Like the Watermeads, Paper Mill Cut lies wholly within what was the parish of Morden, the present course taken by the main stream of the Wandle following roughly the old parish boundary. Maps show the course of the river to have been diverted from time to time, but since the completion of flood control works by Surrey County Council in the early 1960s, when the present automatic gates were installed and a millpond on the north bank was filled in, the Wandle has returned to its ancient channel. During the engineering works one of two old cast-iron parish boundary posts, marked on the OS maps, seems to have been displaced and buried. The other re-emerged in 2004 during site clearance prior to redevelopment of the land behind the Grove Mill building.

## The 'Jack Pond'

Abutting the west bank of the mill cut, within the Watermeads, lies what was known in the late 19th century as the 'Jack Pond', presumably because it once contained pike. The date it was dug and by whom is a little uncertain, but it seems more than likely that it was created to provide an additional reservoir of water for the paper mill. An assured head and volume of water was vital for prolonged operation, and other examples are known, one upstream in Mitcham and two at Merton, where 18th-century mill owners constructed similar large ponds to augment existing millheads, thereby reducing dependency on the river itself when their mills were working.

In the harsh winters around the end of the 19th century the Jack Pond acquired popularity with local 'society' as a place for skating, and Tom Francis remembered Bourne, when he was water bailiff, hanging Chinese lanterns in the trees to give light for parties from the big houses. "Presumably", observed Tom, he "augmented his income and kept himself busy when other work was frozen out."[10] During the inter-war years the pond was allowed to become much overgrown, and degenerated into "a mere swamp". In 1943 the National Trust began reclamation work, removing decayed willows and other overhanging trees and partially cleaning the pond to secure its return to some semblance of its former state.

As we have seen, following further clearance of vegetation and accumulated silt in 1977, the pond was restocked with coarse fish, and for nearly 20 years provided members of Mitcham Angling Club with sport in near-idyllic surroundings. Today the level in the Jack Pond is maintained by a sluice in the bank of the cut, near the point at which it leaves the main river. The sluice itself is fitted with a movable grill to arrest floating debris, and slats to control the level of water. Duckweed presents a major problem, to combat which, by increasing the flow of water, both inlet and outlet channels to the pond were widened and deepened in 2003. Dredging of the pond – the first time since the 1970s – is scheduled for 2005.

## Inter-War Planting

For the quarter century following donation of the Watermeads to the Trust their care would appear to have been in the hands of a voluntary local committee, whose policy seems to have been very much one of *laissez faire* in the belief that, in the main, nature was best left to care for itself. The wisdom of this policy is questionable, and the damp woodland typifying the Watermeads today bears no resemblance to the open meadows dotted with clumps of mature trees glimpsed in Edwardian postcards. In the early years of the 20th century, part of the Watermeads was planted as an osier bed. There were, as Tom Francis, writing in 1946, recalled:

> "two plantations of the Cricket Bat Willow - Salix Coerulea - [and] also several old trees growing on the river bank - these are all the property of a firm of bat makers and some are now ready for felling. During the war it was reported that a bomb had dropped in the plantation among the willows. Last year (1945) soldiers took the matter in hand, built a Bailey bridge over the Wandle to carry their lorries and tackle. The bomb proved to be a dud shell."[11]

The nearby Morden Hall estate was left to the National Trust in 1941 under the terms of the will of Gilliat Edward Hatfeild, and the Watermeads came under the care of Thomas Moore, the Trust's superintendent, who was based at Morden Hall. Access was restricted to keyholders, who were charged a nominal fee. This remained the situation until 2002, since when keys have been more widely available on individual application to the Trust's Morden Hall office.

During the 1940s there developed an interest not only in protecting existing bird life and encouraging nesting, but also in increasing the visual attractions of the Watermeads by introducing ornamental trees and shrubs, and others which, by their berries or foliage, it was hoped would add to the autumn colour. To these ends a number of new varieties were planted, including non-indigenous species and others not normally found in a wetland environment. A leading light in this activity was Tom Francis, a member of the original River Wandle Open Spaces Committee, who was to remain an active member of the Trust until shortly before his death in 1953 at the age of 80. His lecture notes, left to the Borough Council with his collection of lantern slides on 'Old Mitcham', afford a revealing insight into the aspirations shared by many of his contemporaries, as the following excerpts show:

> "Hobson in 'The Book of the Wandle' gives a most interesting list of birds which have been noted in the Wandle Valley - over 80. And it is especially interesting to Mitcham people to learn that no less than 75 of these have been spotted in the Wandle area of Mitcham. J. N. Cheshire, who ran nurseries at Brooklands, near the river, was a bird photographer, ... gave me this information. His observations covered the five years 1928 - 1933. I hope that the National Trust - Watermeads property will still be maintained as a bird sanctuary and as a home for many wild flowers and that in years to come many more interesting trees will grow in this area. The local Committee is doing a bit and hopes, with monetary help from the public, to be able to do a lot more.
>
> "On Saturday last, [Nov. 13th 1943] the Mitcham Civic Society, led by Alderman Gaston (Chairman) planted 17 trees in Watermeads. The trees and their sites had been selected by Thos. Francis (Chairman) of the Local Committee of the National Trust, Mitcham Properties, and Thomas Moore, the Superintendent of Morden Hall Park and Watermeads. The first tree was planted by the Mayoress, Mrs. Jeffery, assisted by the Deputy Mayoress. Alderman Gaston planted a Beech, and Walter Hunt, a veteran sailor of 85, planted an Oak. I planted a Poplar and my wife, a Maple. The other trees were: Purple Beech, Birch, Mountain Ash, Red Chestnut, Tuliptree, Wild Cherry, Catalpa, Red Thorn, Viburnum, Prunus, Common Broom, Hazel and Sumach,

to give colour to the hedges. They were paid for by some members of the Civic Society, and by audiences at "Talks on Old Mitcham". I supplied last winter, a Hawthorn Hedge and standard coloured Thorns, Planes and some Taxodium ditischum (Swamp Cypress). There is a fine one in Happy Valley and also some good gnarled Oaks. About a dozen Poplars in Happy Valley were also supplied by me. Six of them are now growing well and likewise a Hawthorn Hedge near them. Other Poplars were destroyed.

"[Jan. 9th, 1946.] Watermead Trees.

This afternoon, Miss Milnes and 7 Senior Boys from the Boys County School, Lilleshall Road, St. Helier, planted 8 trees (6 in Watermeads and 2 in Happy Valley.) J. H. Moore selected the position. I told the boys that after 6 years of destruction it was a good thing to add a little beauty to the world. We wanted Watermeads to become a home for wild birds, trees and flowers and as they had planted trees today they should be their guardians and discourage wanton destruction.

Larch was planted by R. Hobbs.
White Mulberry by T. Staton and D. Edwards.
Red Oak by T. Horton and D. Clements.
Honey Locust by A. Collins and W. Morgan.
Laburnum (purple) Miss Milnes.

"Jan. 1947. Watermeads Committee again planted trees on the Trust property.

| | |
|---|---|
| Miss Farewell Jones | Lime |
| T. Francis | Prunus |
| F. Blackstone | Other trees. |
| H. H. Dance | Maples. |
| F. S. Buck (Hon. Sec.) | Lime. |
| S. Beven | Prunus |
| T. W. Moore | Staphylea |

T.W.M. said Kingfishers were still there. Shoals of minnows were in the river. A swan and moorhens were seen. Photo of planting published in Advertiser." [12]

## Current Management Policy[13]

Today the Watermeads are managed by the National Trust as a nature reserve, and in order to minimise disturbance of breeding birds, and to protect the somewhat fragile ecosystem, public access to the Watermeads is restricted. No ball games, dogs, vehicles, radios etc. are allowed.

There is generally a greater awareness now than in the past of the special nature of the wetland environment provided by the Watermeads, and opinions as to what species of trees are appropriate when replanting have altered radically in the last 60 years. A few of the specimens planted in the 1940s may still be found, notably around the glade which marks the site of the paper mill, but over much of the area self-sown sycamores predominate, with willow and Italian black poplar two other prominent species. There is also a dense undergrowth of bramble and scrub.

Like much of southern England, the Trust's Wandle properties suffered considerable damage during the great storm of October 1987. Many old and mature trees were toppled and several others damaged. Clearance of fallen timber from the Watermeads took several years. Management is now directed towards routine scrub clearance, leaving behind much of the fallen timber, smaller branches and brushwood to provide useful habitats for fungi and insects, as well as cover for small mammals. Inevitably, soil disturbance and the removal of former tree cover has encouraged a rampant growth of willow herb and thistle, together with invasive exotics such as Himalayan balsam and Japanese knotweed, all of which need to be controlled, or in some cases eradicated where they threaten to dominate indigenous vegetation or distort the ecological balance to an unacceptable degree. A recent addition to the list of 'undesirables' is the native marsh pennywort.

Whereas in the south-eastern part of the Watermeads regeneration of the natural cover of alder and willow carr is encouraged, in 1993 it was jointly agreed by the National Rivers Authority and the Trust that in the low-lying area between the mill cut and the main river an attempt should be made to recreate a watermeadow-type habitat. This policy continues, with the Environment Agency (successor to the NRA) supporting the Trust's objectives. With a naturally high water table the land still supports a variety of wetland plants, including several species now relatively uncommon in the London area. Reliance has been placed on the seed bank remaining in the soil for re-colonisation.

Since 1998, when an influx of 'travellers' with their caravans caused considerable nuisance, security against unauthorised entry to the Watermeads has perforce become an important element in the Trust's management strategy. Partly for economic reasons, annual mowing of Morden Meadow to produce a hay crop has ceased, and grass cutting is kept to a minimum consistent with providing authorised access, preferably after the seeds have ripened and been shed. The resultant stand of tall grasses and wild flowers does seem to have proved less inviting to unwanted visitors.

For many years the paths along the bank of the river, beside Paper Mill Cut, and leading to the 'Jack Pond', were kept mown for the benefit of visitors. During the spring of 1993 a new meandering path was cut through the taller vegetation by volunteers from the London Wildlife Trust, to give improved access through the centre of the property. This, it was intended, would be kept open, to develop eventually into a grassy ride widening to small open areas of grassland attractive to small mammals and their predators. Recently this plan has been modified in favour of creating a circular walk, and to this end a bridge erected over Paper Mill Cut during the winter of 1994/5 was overhauled and repaired. By coincidence, the bridge occupies the site of a far earlier bridge, marked on the 1894 Ordnance Survey map.

An ancient sluice gate in the northern bank of the mill cut was repaired by the National Rivers Authority in 1994, making it possible once more to control flooding of the wetland between the cut and the main river. Old channels were cleared out, and at the southern end of the area, where a small pond already existed, a reed bed of *phragmites communis*, the tallest of our native perennial grasses, has been encouraged to develop. In addition to creating a special habitat attractive to wetland species of birds, this rush bed also traps suspended particulate matter in the water flowing into the area, assisting in its purification and contributing to the enhancement of the river quality downstream. Maintenance is essential to the success of this regime, and currently the Trust is working with the Environment Agency clearing the channels of ten years' accumulation of sediment and vegetation.

*The south side of Nos 475–479 London Road, seen from Morden Meadow May 1967 (ENM)*

# Chapter 4

## THE MILL COTTAGES (Nos. 475 - 479 London Road)

In a picturesque setting to the east of Mitcham Bridge, upstream from where the road crosses the river Wandle, there stands a group of three weatherboarded houses. By the 1980s they were sadly dilapidated, but they survived, and now have a potential for becoming attractive properties. The site they occupy was once an island, created by the diversion of the Wandle to serve precursors of what were known latterly as the Grove and Crown mills. The river ceased to be used for power over half a century ago, and the mill pond and various channels have been filled in, leaving the Wandle today to follow a course not so very different from that which existed in the Middle Ages.

The double-fronted house facing the bridge is a comparative newcomer, built shortly after 1851, but its companions date in part to the middle of the 18th century, and on this account are increasingly rare survivals in this part of Greater London of a style of vernacular architecture once common throughout north-eastern Surrey and Kent. Each was built of timber-framing clad externally in overlapping deal weather-boarding, a remarkably durable and resilient form of construction much in vogue between about 1750 and 1800, and persisting locally until about 1850. The internal finish was in lath and plaster or tongue-and-groove boarding. A simple concave canopy in the 'chinoiserie' style of the late Regency period covers the front door to the central cottage, whilst the oldest of the group is symmetrically double-fronted in the Georgian fashion and enjoys the added distinction of possessing bow windows with sliding boxed sashes to the original pattern. The roofs are covered either with slates, plain tiles or pantiles which, with a medley of outbuildings and extensions, serve to underline the *ad hoc* nature of development on the site.

Two cottages are recorded in the earliest surviving Mitcham poor rate book, which dates from 1755,[1] and although much altered since then, the two houses, numbered 477 and 479, today probably incorporate within their structure parts of these early buildings. Whereas it has not been confirmed, the erection of the third of the houses, numbered 475 London Road, can probably be attributed to Richard Jones, a felt manufacturer who, around the middle of the 19th century, acquired the then empty Crown snuff mill and adapted it for his own use.[2] Despite their somewhat ramshackle appearance, the importance of the two older houses from an architectural and historical point of view was first recognised by the Ministry of Housing and Local Government in 1952, and they were afforded a Grade III listing. The value of the group as a screen obscuring what was, until recently, an unsightly collection of sheds and industrial buildings from the view of visitors to the National Trust's Watermeads property, has also long been recognised by the local planning authorities. With the addition of No. 475 the three former mill cottages now have a listing of Grade II on the statutory list.[3] They are also within the London Borough of Merton's Wandle Valley Conservation Area.

Until the close of the 19th century all three cottages were occupied by mill owners, managers or mill workers. As we have noted earlier, from about 1895 No 475 – Wandle Cottage – was tenanted for a few years by Henry Bourne, bailiff of a short-lived private angling association. By 1907 it had become the residence of a Mr Seager, who had taken over part of the Crown Mill for manufacturing purposes, and by the insertion of a door in the party wall with No. 477 he converted the two houses into one. Seager's stay in Britain ended with the outbreak of war in 1914, and he returned to his native Holland. No. 477 reverted to being a separate dwelling, occupied by a Mr Eilers, and he was followed by the Gibb family, who made the house their home for some 40 years. No. 475 also reverted to its original role as a separate dwelling, and became for a while the residence of a Mr Cooper, the proprietor of a corn and coal business in the London Road opposite the former Kings Head (now the Burn Bullock).[4] Until quite recently it had a succession of tenants, most of them connected with the mills. Like the other houses, it is now owner-occupied.

The building of No. 479 London Road may be attributable to Edward Nash, who held the lease of the flour mill in the mid-18th century. It continued to be occupied either by the proprietor or manager of the Grove Mill until Ashby Brothers' lease expired in 1902 and the long history of corn milling in Mitcham came to an end. The mill building itself was soon taken over by the expanding Patent Horse Hair Company

*No 475 London Road in 1910 (above) and in the 1930s (below)*
*(Photographs reproduced by courtesy of Merton Library Service)*

*No 479 London Road, the oldest of the three mill cottages, May 1967*
*This view is the front of the cottage which faces north. (ENM)*

*No 479 London Road from the east, as seen from the Crown Mill in the 1930s*
*(Photograph reproduced by courtesy of Merton Library Service)*

from the nearby Crown Mill, and for many years No. 479 was used partly as an office and partly as the residence of the firm's foreman, John Smith, and afterwards by his successor, a Mr Kemp.[4]

In view of their individual character as well as their group value, in 1954 all three houses were placed on the Ministry of Housing and Local Government's Supplementary List of buildings of special architectural or historic interest. When the firm of C S Walker (Sacks) Ltd purchased the vacant Crown Mill at auction 1959 it was not immediately appreciated that the property included three occupied houses, let at controlled rents. Whilst their quaint appearance and historic interest were appreciated, the company did not intend to spend money on their maintenance, apart from what was received in rent, and as a consequence the condition of all three properties steadily deteriorated. Eventually No. 479, occupied by an elderly woman with an unauthorised sub-tenant - a young woman with a baby, in 1966 attracted the attention of a health visitor from the Borough Council. By now the house was in such a state of disrepair that it was unfit, and on the criteria then used by local authorities could not be considered repairable at reasonable expense. On the recommendation of its public health committee in July 1967 Merton Council placed a closing order on the property, and re-housed the tenant and sub-tenant.

By virtue of the listing the owners were deterred from considering demolition as an option, and for several years No. 479, affected by dry rot and its condition steadily worsening, was merely used for the storage of sacking. With vacant possession however, the building had acquired a much enhanced value, despite the need for substantial repairs, and it was finally purchased for owner-occupation, the new owner embarking on a programme of extensive rehabilitation which, in the event, resulted virtually in a complete rebuilding. In 1993 the much improved house was offered for sale at £150,000 as 'Fisheries Cottage' – a name for which there is no historical justification - and now, once more owner-occupied, it is an attractive member of the group. No. 477 also became owner-occupied and has been renovated, but No. 475 remained in the possession of C S Walker Ltd, and was tenanted by one of the firm's employees. It, too, was redecorated externally after substantial repairs by the company in 1993, and was sold in 1997. The new owners were confronted with extensive decay in the structural timbers, and embarked on a long programme of rehabilitation.

Probably more film and artists' canvas has been expended on recording the mill houses than any other buildings in the Borough. Aesthetically charming, and intimately connected with the Wandle and the industries which once depended on the river, they have survived to provide an important thread of continuity through over two and a half centuries of change. With the protection of statutory listing their future seems a little more secure and, given owners appreciative of their unique character and able to keep them in good repair, it is to be hoped they will continue to occupy the site for a good many years to come.

*Grove Mill, Crown Mill and 475 London Road viewed from Mitcham Bridge shortly before 1907, when fire severely damaged Grove Mill (Photograph reproduced by courtesy of Merton Library Service)*

# Chapter 5

# THE MILLS BY MITCHAM BRIDGE

## Early History

The Domesday survey recorded two mills in Mitcham in 1086, both of which were working at the time of King Edward the Confessor.[1] One was described as being in 'Whitford', or Lower Mitcham, and the other appears to have been located downstream at Phipps Bridge. The majority of mills at this period were used for the grinding of cereals, and the evidence points to the Wandle, which in the half mile between Willow Lane and Mitcham bridge has a fall of about six feet, having been exploited as a source of power well before the Norman Conquest. Since then numerous industries have come and gone along this stretch of river, one of the last to survive being that of corn milling. Other activities included the bleaching and printing of linen and cotton fabrics, colour or 'drug' milling, copper working, paper making, snuff milling, the manufacture of felt and, most recently, of materials for use in upholstery.

*Crown Mill, 475 London Road and Morden snuff mill, c.1906*
*(Photograph reproduced by courtesy of Merton Library Service)*

During the 1960s infilling of the large mill pond behind the Grove and Crown mills on the north bank of the river upstream from Mitcham bridge finally ended this long history of industrial use, and within a few years only the Grove mill building survived, although its occupiers no longer relied upon the Wandle for power, and none of the milling machinery remained. Planning consent for conversion of the mill to create flats, and redevelopment of vacant land to the rear for housing, was approved by the local authority, and work commenced with site clearance in 2004.

The Grove mill building, its name derived from the mill's having become part of the Mitcham Grove estate by the 17th century, probably stands close to the site of Whitford mill. In King Edward's time this was owned by a Saxon called Lank but, following the Conquest, it passed into the hands of William FitzAnsculf, one of the great Norman landlords, and subsequently to the de Mara family. By the mid-12th century Whitford mill was in the possession of the de Whitford family, to whom part of FitzAnsculf's Domesday holding in Lower Mitcham had been granted. Members of the de Whitford, or 'Witford', family, who were prominent in Lower Mitcham during the 12th and 13th centuries, made several bequests to the newly established priory of St Mary at Southwark. Amongst them was Alexander de Witford who, between 1200 and 1230, confirmed the presentation of the tithes of his mill to the prior and canons "for the love of God and the salvation of my soul and of my ancestors and descendants".[2]

The de Witfords held part of their lands in Mitcham as feudal tenants of the de Mara, or Mareys, family,[3] and what may be assumed to be the Whitford mill was one of the two mills included in the estate in 'Wickford' which William Mareys conveyed to the Church in 1362.[4] The prior of Merton was said to be holding the 'manor' of Wickford when an inquiry was held in 1380,[5] and Malden suggested that Mareys's gift may have been in trust for the priory.[6] This could well have been the case, and land known variously as 'Mareyslond', 'Mareshlandes', 'Marish' or 'Marshfee', lying partly in Lower Mitcham and extending south of the Wandle into Carshalton, was amongst the possessions of Merton priory at the time of the Dissolution.

During the later Middle Ages it became common practice for property belonging to the great monastic houses to be leased or 'farmed' to tenants. The estate of Westminster Abbey at Morden was managed in this way,[7] and records surviving from before the Dissolution show the same policy being followed by Merton priory.[8] Thus in his will dated January 1529/30 William Standon, or Stondon, 'Yeoman of the Crown', mentioned "all my lease from Merton Priory in Mitcham called Marrisfeeland" and his 'capital messuage' called 'Mares Garden' in Mitcham.[9] At the Dissolution, according to the *Victoria County History* the prior was in receipt of £3 1s 8d "as the farm of land called Maresland",[10] and in the account of John Bowland, collector of rents in 1538, "certain land called Mareshlandes in Micham and Carshalton" held by Merton Priory were yielding £3 11s 8d.[11] No records seem to have survived to show what happened to Whitford mill during the 15th and early 16th centuries, but both the Grove Mill and its neighbour the Crown Mill, occupying the site in the 19th century, were recorded as 'tithe free' in the survey conducted for the tithe commissioners in 1846, which is consistent with the early mills having been in the tenure of the Church during the Middle Ages.[12]

In 1544 Robert Wylford, or Wilford, a merchant in the City of London, was granted 'in fee-farm' several estates formerly belonging to Merton Priory including the 'Mareslondes', or 'Mares-fee' land in Mitcham "late in the occupation of William Standon".[13] Following Wilford's death the following year this freehold property passed to his heirs and was subsequently sold. Amongst those buying portions of the former Wilford estate was Thomas Smythe, to whom reference as a resident of Mitcham first occurs in 1564.[14] Smythe was a high-ranking official in Queen Elizabeth's government, and the owner of extensive estates, including land in Mitcham and Wandsworth, where he held the lordship of the manor of Dunsford, and another manor in Wiltshire.[15] A "Micham mille" finds mention in 1572 when maintenance work on the river was called for by the Surrey and Kent Sewer Commissioners, but its precise location is not made clear in the published minutes.[16] From later records, however, it would appear to have been a forerunner of the Grove mill and was, presumably, then in Smythe's possession. In his will, dated 1575, he left the major portion of his estate, including his "choice house and Landes" in Mitcham, to his wife Elenor (*sic*) and their son George, then aged 14.[17] The boy duly inherited much of his father's property, including the "howse by the Watersyd", which in later years became known as Mitcham Grove.[15] As a young man George Smythe set about enlarging his estate, purchasing various freehold properties in Lower Mitcham and elsewhere,[18] and by the reign of James I he had become a major landowner and a prominent local figure.[19]

In 1610 George Smythe was recorded as owning three mills on the Wandle.[20] Exactly where they were is not stated, but one of them must have been the "Micham mille" mentioned 40 years previously. It is also likely to have been the "Cornmill" which was referred to as "Micham Mill alias Wickford Mill alias Marris Mill" in an indenture dated 1645 detailing lands offered as security when Thomas Smythe, George's son, was raising a loan.[21] The mill was described as having a "high drying room or loft adjoining and two closes of marsh ground" and, most importantly, it was made clear that it was "all in the parish of Mitcham". This places the mill building north of the river, which in the vicinity of Mitcham bridge defined the boundary between Mitcham and the adjoining parishes of Morden and Carshalton.

In 1584, during George Smythe's minority and when the family estates were in the care of his mother and her second husband, Dr Bartholomew Clerk, two water mills and 30 acres called the 'Marish' in Mitcham featured in a dispute over manorial rights between Sir Francis Carew of Beddington (who had been granted lordship of the manor of Ravensbury in 1554) and Charles Howard, Baron Howard of Effingham (Elizabeth I's Lord High Admiral at the time of the Armada), who held the manor of Reigate.[22] Exactly where these mills stood is not known for certain but, since as late as 1940 a quit rent of 20 shillings per annum was still being claimed by the manor of Reigate from Mitcham Hair and Fibre Mills, then the owners of the Grove Mill and the adjoining Crown Mill, it is a reasonable assumption that one or both of them occupied the site of one of the 16th century mills. Reigate's claim was probably well-founded but in September 1940 the Battle of Britain was at its height, and the manor steward was politely informed by the managing director of the Mitcham Hair and Fibre Mills that

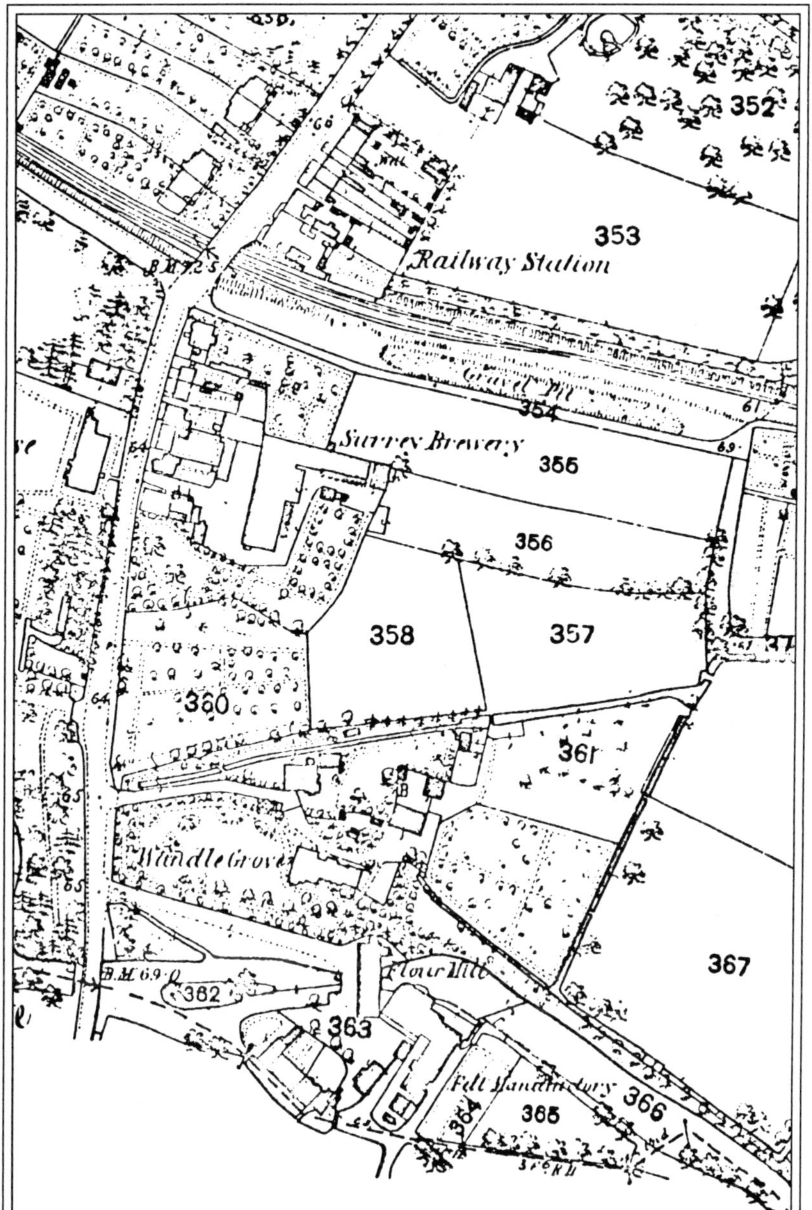


*Detail from Ordnance Survey 25-inch map of 1867*

consideration of the claim would have to be deferred. In the event, the matter was never resolved.[23]

Over the succeeding centuries the mills were enlarged, burned down, rebuilt and extended. The peak of industrial activity was reached at the beginning of the 19th century, but then, with the gradual adoption of steam power, industry was no longer restricted to riverside sites and steadily migrated to other locations. The end came very slowly in Mitcham, however, and in the short stretch of the Wandle between Willow Lane and Ravensbury four large mills continued working until after the 1914-18 war. The great iron wheel of the Grove Mill was one of the last to see service, and proved invaluable during the harsh winter of 1947 when a power crisis forced many other works to suspend production. In the mid-1960s diversion of the Wandle by Surrey County Council rendered the wheel redundant, and it was dismantled. By the 1980s only the Grove mill building remained, its yellow stock bricks regrettably disfigured by the ill-advised application of white paint. Of the nearby Crown Mill, which was destroyed by fire in 1964, nothing survived to be seen above ground.

## Copper Milling (1698-*c.*1748)

Surveys of the manor of Reigate conducted in the 17th century continued to list amongst properties within the manor's jurisdiction a tenement and water mill and 30 acres of 'marsh ground' at Mitcham, for which a yearly rent of 20 shillings was paid by the freeholders, the Smythes.[1] Its location is not made clear but, as already stated, a case may be made for the property to have included the site of either the Grove or Crown mills. In the list of freeholders compiled during surveys dated *c.* 1701-1707 is the entry "Smith of Mitcham, widow, claimeth to hold of this manor one messuage or tenement with a water mill now used for the working of copper, and a parcel of marsh ground thereunto belonging, situate and being at Mitcham, conteining 30 acres 1 rood 9 perches, at £1 quit rent".[2] Clearly, the same property was involved in both cases and, with its associated land, buildings and appurtenances, it remained a distinct holding until 1768, when it was sold by William Myers, by whom it had been inherited.[3]

The water mill held by Mrs Smith early in the 17th century seems to have been the copper works at Mitcham known as the Tower Mills, which Thomas Cletscher, a Swedish traveller, noted in 1698. The works comprised a small re-melting furnace, a rolling mill and a forge, and it was a condition of its licence that only native copper should be used.[4] A monopoly in copper manufacture which had existed in this country collapsed during the Civil War, and after the formation of the English Copper Company in 1691 the industry expanded. A number of new battery and rolling mills, for which water power was the only practicable source of energy, were established in England in the late 17th century, often employing the skills of Dutch metalworkers, and copper mills began to proliferate along the Wandle valley at this time. A change in use of one of the Mitcham mills from corn milling to the working of copper, or its alloys bronze and brass, could well be ascribed to the same period.

The name of the actual proprietor of the copper mill at Mitcham was not given by Cletscher, nor was it recorded in the court rolls, but it was most probably Charles Perry (or Parry) who is said to have obtained (or renewed) a licence to manufacture copper coins (or more likely blanks) at the Tower Mills in 1712. A Francis Parry was a partner at a copper smelting works established by the English Copper Company on the river Wye at Redbrook in about 1691, and it is reasonable to assume the two men were related. The family's Mitcham roots may go back to the mid-17th century, when a James Perry, who died in 1659 and was described as a 'whitster', citizen and leather-seller of London, held the position of high constable for Wallington during the Commonwealth.[5]

It is understood that, according to the records of St Paul's Cathedral, the original ball and cross were made at "Andrew Niblett's copper mill at Mitcham" in 1708, but this mill has not been identified and there seems to be no mention of Niblett in Mitcham parish records. Niblett died in August 1736, and all one can conclude is that his presence in Mitcham was of short duration, and that he was buried elsewhere. Niblett is said to have been paid £1,538 1s 6d "for ye Balle and Crosse for ye lantern". It withstood the atmosphere of London for about 100 years, and was taken down in 1821 and replaced with the present ball and

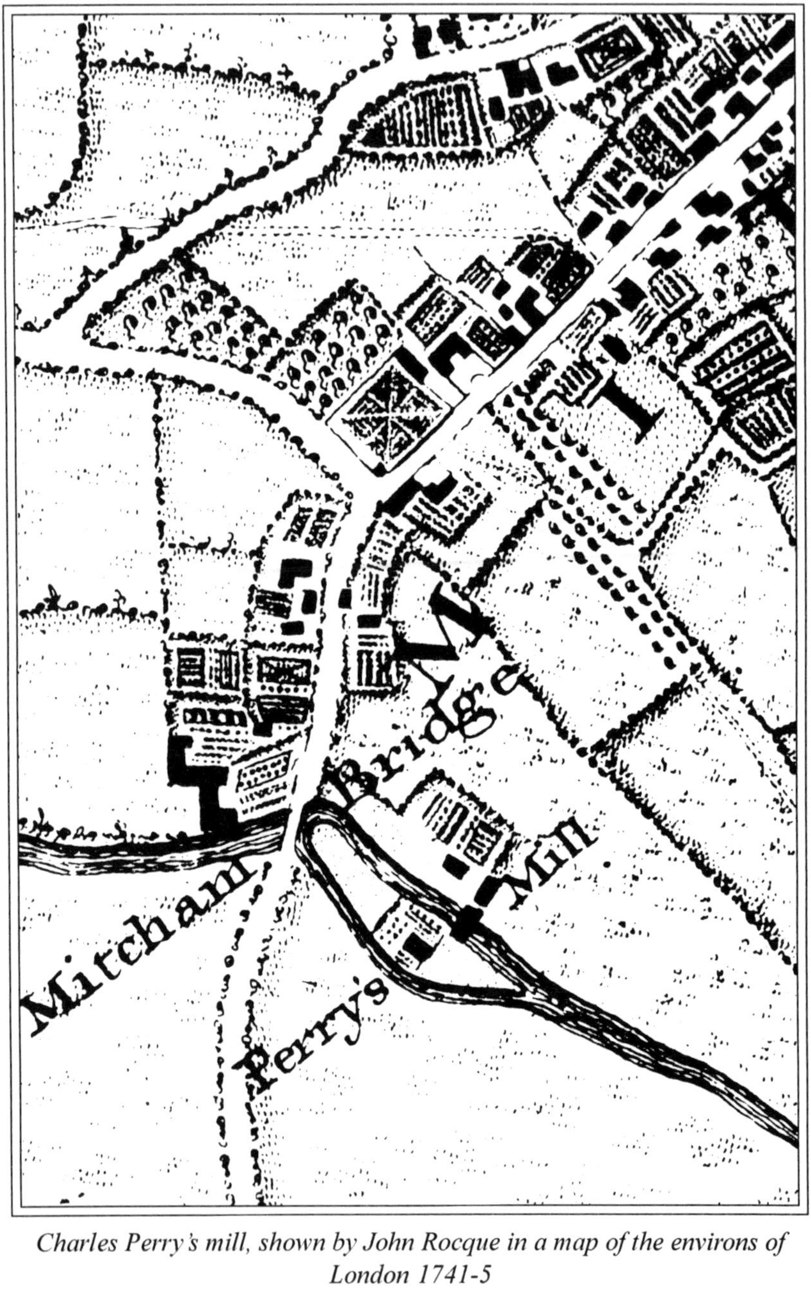


*Charles Perry's mill, shown by John Rocque in a map of the environs of London 1741-5*

cross.[6] By the mid-1720s copper working had evidently declined at Mitcham, for Henrich Karlmeter, another Swede, did not see fit to include the Tower Mills amongst the six he listed, merely referring to a "works of former importance at Mitcham".[4]

Ownership of Perry's mill and the rest of the estate had passed to William Myers in 1725 under the terms of Susannah Smythe's will, and remained in the ownership of his family throughout the second quarter of the 18th century.[7] On the evidence of a ledgerstone inscribed to the memory of a Charles "Parry" in the central aisle of Mitcham parish church, Perry seems to have died in 1748. On his map of the environs of London, dated 1741-5, John Rocque had marked "Perry's Mill" close by Mitcham Bridge, and in an indenture dated March 1764, when the mill and associated buildings and land were being sold, reference was made to "ground on (the) south side of buildings with the three small messuages/ tenements and a barn thereon standing all in Mitcham, ... late in the occupation of Charles Perry deceased".[8] There is also mention of a house and garden with three acres of land, which could well have been his residence. A deed of sale was completed four years later, when the former Smythe property was purchased by Rowland Frye of Wallington. By this time the old Tower Mill building seems to have been either converted or, more likely, demolished and completely rebuilt, for it is described in the deeds as "a millhouse and 3 water corn mills therein".[3] As "Mitcham Mill" this is shown in a later map produced by Rocque, published in the mid-1760s.

## The Flour Mills (1765-1795)

In 1765, prior to completion of sale of the freehold of Mitcham Mill to Rowland Frye, a fresh lease was granted to the existing lessee, Edward Nash.[1] A miller, he was already in occupation of what the indenture makes clear were three cornmills "within one building". As we have seen, in addition to the "millhouse" or mill building, which we can assume occupied the site of the later Grove Mill, the lease included cottages, a barn and land formerly leased by Perry. The earliest Mitcham poor rate books to survive show Nash assessed for rates in respect of a mill near Mitcham Bridge as far back as 1756, but whether this was

Perry's mill, or a new building, it is impossible to say.[2] It does, nevertheless, seem likely Nash had taken over the lease of the premises, perhaps a decade or so earlier and soon after Perry's retirement. The deeds also mention a house, with a garden and yard, plus two closes of land, but apart from making it clear the premises were in Mitcham, there is nothing to show exactly where they stood, nor anything to suggest this was where Nash lived. (It is tempting, however, to believe it was close to the mill, perhaps on the site in Riverside Drive now occupied by Wandle House.) By 1765, Nash was evidently on the point of vacating the premises, for they were then described as "now or late Edward Nash".[3]

William Myers, who was selling the property, was a graduate of Lincoln College, Oxford, and had been born in about 1713. His father, an attorney, died in 1742 and, like him, William also followed a career in law.[4] The sale of the freehold title provides an interesting example of the tortuous conveyancing procedure customary in the 18th century and, it might be said, of the means by which many members of the legal profession secured a comfortable living. Disposal of the property commenced in March 1764 with the sale by Archibald Stewart and William Myers of a year's lease to Robert Cochran, an apothecary of Scottish birth then living in a house overlooking Mitcham's Cricket Green.[5] Stewart, a London wine merchant and former MP for Edinburgh, was resident at 'Mitcham Grove', the impressive mansion on the banks of the Wandle which had been in the ownership of the Smythes since the late 16th century. His involvement in the transaction probably stemmed from his holding a sub-lease of the Grove estate from Myers. In August 1765 Cochran and John Marlar, another London merchant, granted Nash two "leases" (probably sub-leases) of land and mills for a period of 99 years.[6] The freehold of the land (in this case only part seems to have been involved) was conveyed by Cochran to Rowland Frye in October 1768 by the grant of a year's lease, followed shortly afterwards by the sale of the reversionary interest.[7] Marlar's father, a "citizen and haberdasher of London", had been a prominent calico printer early in the century, and was buried at Beddington. John, who was styled "of Beddington, Cheapside and Mitcham", was living in another of Myers's properties, a substantial house, previously the residence of William Myers himself, in Lower Mitcham.[8] There is no evidence to suggest that either Cochran or Marlar were in any way concerned with the actual processes at the mill, and their involvement in the transactions is likely to have been entirely as intermediaries.

It so happens that a considerable number of documents, both private and public, survive from the latter part of the 18th century recording the various changes of tenure of the mills by Mitcham bridge. It has to be admitted, however, that they can be somewhat baffling, since it is not always obvious to which premises they referred. An added difficulty is that a mill building may have contained more than one mill, or set of stones, a subtlety not always made clear. This applies particularly to the earliest continuous and reasonably detailed local government records to have survived for Mitcham – the parochial rate books and, from 1780, the land tax records – which, although quite adequate for their original purposes, can confuse the unwary researcher.

From the rate books one finds that John Chesterman, a flour miller, was in occupation of a house and one of the three mills by Mitcham bridge in the late 1760s.[9] In 1772 Edward Nash, whose name is recorded in the 1756 rate book, granted to a Lionel Gregory, who was also described as "of Mitcham, miller," a sub-lease for 91 years at £85 per quarter of the upper part of his "corn mill near Mitcham bridge".[10] The lease included a second house and land, a conduit and water-gate, and specific mention was made of the right of access to and from the Mitcham high road. (The private roadway giving access to the Grove Mill building and the former mill cottages still exists.) Detailed conditions were laid down regarding future maintenance of the mill and, most importantly, control and use of water. The schedule to Gregory's lease is of additional interest, for it refers to "that part of the mills now or late used as a snuff mill" - the first mention we have of snuff milling at this locality - and describes the wheels and milling machinery in some detail. Gregory's tenure was of short duration, however, and within two years his lease was assigned by his executors to Richard Glover, who was described as a "mealman".

From valuations made by Mitcham parish officers for rating purposes it can be deduced (somewhat tentatively) that Nash sub-leased the largest and most valuable of the three mills to Gregory and Chesterman, retaining what seems to have been only a small part of the premises for his own use. The easternmost of the three houses standing today, No. 479 London Road, seems to have been his residence until about 1776, when he appears to have retired from milling, and in 1780 he is to be found in the land tax records as living at Tamworth Lodge, a more substantial house overlooking Mitcham Common.[11] Next to Richard Glover, who had moved into Nash's former house, were John Chesterman and his family, who remained there until the early 1790s. Research into insurance policies has disclosed that Chesterman was also involved in brewing, and from 1774 until 1784 he was in partnership with William Hughes of the nearby Globe Brewery.[12]

Edward Nash had married Mary, a daughter of John and Ann Glover of Norwood, members of the influential Glover family.[13] A branch of the Glovers had been living in Mitcham for many years, and a Gabriel Glover, described as "of London, linen draper", was resident with his wife and children in a large house in Lower Mitcham (later known as Baron House) from the 1680s until about 1720. Various members of the family are buried in the parish church, where at least one memorial to them remains visible in the south aisle.[14]

Mary Nash predeceased Edward by some 30 years,[15] and when he died tenure of the smaller mill passed to Richard Glover, who seems to have been Edward Nash's nephew.[16] The precise relationship has not been verified, but an older Richard Glover, who may have been Mary's brother, is recorded in the court rolls of the manor of Carshalton as having died between 1765 and 1769. Richard Glover junior, who was described as a "mealman" in one document, had been in the flour milling business at Mitcham since about 1774, when he took over the sub-lease of Gregory's mill. He evidently set about enlarging or rebuilding Nash's mill soon after acquiring possession, for within a few years his assessment for land tax increased four-fold. In July 1789 Glover insured his "brick, timber and tiled dwelling house" (No. 479 London Road) with the Sun Insurance Co., for £300, and his "Water Corn Millhouse" nearby for £700. Its contents, stock and utensils were covered for a like amount. The millhouse was built of brick and timber and, rather surprisingly for a concern so vulnerable to fire, was "cover'd with Tarr'd

Paper and Gravel".[17] As might be expected, given his business interests and family connections, Richard Glover was regarded as a man of some standing in the community, and was an active member of Mitcham vestry for many years. He was elected overseer of the poor for the year 1777-1778, and in 1781 was one of the gentlemen whose names were put forward by the vestry to serve as surveyors of highways.[18] In the same year he secured appointment as an assessor for the land tax.

Richard Glover's neighbour, John Chesterman, died in 1784 and tenure of his mill passed to his widow.[19] By his will, proved in February 1784, Chesterman left his share in the brewery to his executors in trust for his son Caleb, who was still a minor.[20] Four years later, when the occupier is given in one source as Samuel Chesterman, their timber and tiled "Mitcham Corn Mill", which seems to have been on the site of the present Grove Mill, was destroyed by fire.[21] Rebuilding took place almost immediately, but Mrs Chesterman and her family must have been left in financial straits, for in 1789 we find the vestry pressing them for non-payment of rates.[18] At this time the three mills and the land on which they stood were owned by Samuel Frye, who had inherited the estate in Mitcham and Carshalton purchased by Rowland Frye in 1774.

It is evident that within a short while the Chestermans' lease was surrendered to Richard Glover, who by 1795 was in possession of all three mills, two used for the grinding of corn and one for snuff, valued together for land tax purposes at £293 per annum - a not inconsiderable sum in those days. This was the situation in 1805, when James Malcolm duly included "Mr. Glover's flour mill" as one of the Wandle mills listed in his *Compendium of Modern Husbandry*, published that year. Malcolm does, however, imply that Glover had sub-leased part of the premises, for immediately following the flour mill he also listed "Mr. Stevenson's snuff mills, all in Mitcham parish".[22]

## The Snuff Mills (1772-1845)

The fact that Sir Walter Raleigh and his wife had owned land in Mitcham, and that he is popularly (if erroneously) credited with the introduction of tobacco into this country, gave rise to a belief locally that it was Sir Walter himself who had brought snuff milling to the Wandle valley. The truth is that in the 16th century tobacco, either for smoking or snuffing, was carried back to Europe by many of the explorers and adventurers returning from the New World. Furthermore, the taking of snuff, although already widespread on the Continent by the end of the century, did not become fashionable in England for another 100 years, long after Sir Walter's death, and seems to have been introduced via Ireland and Scotland. It is puzzling, therefore, that Morden Mill, a little weatherboarded snuff mill which stood on the southern bank of the Wandle above Mitcham Bridge until 1922, should be referred to in some local history notes as "Raleigh's mill" or even, more specifically, "Caleb Raleigh's mill" without, so far as can be ascertained, any justification whatsoever.[1]

As we have seen, there is reference to snuff milling having taken place in one of the mills at Mitcham in the sub-lease granted by Edward Nash to Lionel Gregory in 1772,[2] and Edwards, in about 1789, noted Richard Glover's corn and snuff mills lying to the east of Mitcham bridge.[3] The early snuff mill was in the lower part of the building leased by Nash, but in view of Edwards' assertion that Chesterman's corn mill was destroyed by fire in 1788, it has to be assumed that Glover's snuff mill was in a structually separate part of the millhouse, and survived. Nothing in Edwards' account suggests that another mill stood on the Morden side of the river by 1790, but it would perhaps be better not to rely overmuch on his observations on whatwas a complex arrangement. It is also clear that around the turn of the century considerable changes were taking place, but at this distance in time they appear impossible to unravel.

Henry Hoare had acquired a leasehold interest in the property by 1809, presumably on the termination of Stevenson's tenure, for the records of the Royal Exchange Insurance Co. show that in March a fire insurance policy was taken out by Hoare on the snuff mill on the north bank, then in the occupation of Richard Glover.[4] This may have been newly erected, and the precaution of ensuring adequate cover was eminently sensible for, as recent experience at the flour mill had demonstrated, given the right conditions the dust raised in the milling processes was potentially explosive. Furthermore, Glover's snuff mill was a timber-built structure, "covered with a composition of paper, pitch and gravel" and therefore highly inflammable. For insurance purposes the mill building itself was valued at £1200, and the "standing and going gear, millstones, machinery and utensils therein" were covered for £1000.

Morden poor rate books for the period are of little help in the quest to discover when the snuff mill on the south bank was built, and the Morden land tax records from 1780 until 1831[5] contain no entry at all which specifically relates to a mill, but "Land" valued at £19 p.a., described as "late Nash" under the heading of "Proprietor" and "Richard Glover" under "Occupier", finds a place in the tax book for 1793. Before that an assessment of £19 was listed, but it was not ascribed to land, or anything else. Particulars of tenure given over the 24 years from 1780 to 1804 can be summarised as follows:

| | **Proprietor** | **Occupier** |
|---|---|---|
| 1780-1784 | Edward Nash | Edward Nash |
| 1785 | " " | Richard Glover |
| 1786-1793 | Late Nash | " " |
| 1795-1798 | Henry Hoare | " " |
| 1799-1803 | - Fry | " " |

Then, in 1804, with no change in ownership or occupation being recorded, the assessment increased to £63 per annum, and was sustained at this level until the records ceased in 1831. No reason is given, but the sudden increase in valuation is what one would expect to see if some new development, such as the construction of a mill, had taken place on the land shortly before 1804.

The first positive reference to what in later years was known as 'Morden Mill', is contained in another Royal Exchange Fire Insurance Policy, also dated March 8th 1809, taken out by "Henry Hoare of Fleet Steet, London, Esq." Hoare was the senior partner of the bank of that name, and lived at Mitcham Grove, immediately downstream from Mitcham bridge. The policy was on a "Snuff Millhouse timber and slated situate in the parish of Morden Co. of Surrey, in the occupation of Richard Glover" valued at £300.[6] Cover for the "standing and going gears, millstones and utensils therein" was for £380. The mill is shown on Henry Hoare's estate map of 1812,[7] which would suggest that by this time he held the head-lease of the property. As a leasehold property it was similarly included in a later map, prepared by Edwin Chart, a local surveyor, to accompany the sale particulars of Henry Hoare's estate when it was auctioned as a leasehold property shortly after his death in 1828.[8] In the prospectus the "Paddock by Morden Snuff Mills" was listed and is identifiable as the meadow now owned by the National Trust. The "mills" (the reference is definitely in the plural in the sale particulars, implying that the building contained at least two sets of stones), with two cottages on the Mitcham, or north bank, and stabling, kilns, millwright's shop, piggery and cowsheds, were in the occupation of Richard Glover.

In an account of a perambulation of the bounds of Mitcham by the parish officers in 1833, Chart noted "Morden Mill" as a land mark, and described the land adjoining as "Morden Mill Meadow".[9] The following year the mill was stated to be empty.[10] The records of the Morden tithe commutation survey conducted in 1837/8 list the landowner as Mrs Spencer "(late Fry)", and a Richard Glover as the occupier.[11] In addition to the snuff mill, Glover held the lease of three paddocks in Morden, two "strips", a pond and mill tail, totalling in all three and a half acres. Access to his house on the northern, or Mitcham, bank was by a wooden bridge. Also on the Morden side of the river, and in the hands of John Glover, were a further seven acres, including a "large building" – a disused paper mill to which we will return later.

A draft consignment note for snuff signed by Richard Glover junior for his father, dated February 1835,[12] implies that father and son were in partnership at this time. Glover senior must have been well into his 80s, and we can assume that the Richard Glover whose name was noted in Crawter's survey conducted in 1838 as the occupier of a snuff mill on the northern side of the river was the son, and then running the business.[13] He continued to be listed in the commercial directories for Mitcham from 1839 until 1845, either as a snuff grinder or a snuff and tobacco merchant.[14] The position is not completely clear, however, for by the 1840s a grandson, also named Richard, would have been old enough to have joined the family business. Braithwaite, studying the mills working on the Wandle in the spring of 1853,[15] noted a "small snuff mill" on the south bank, but did not describe its machinery, perhaps because it was no longer in use. It certainly seems a reasonable assumption that from the mid-1830s onwards the Glovers' snuff milling activity was largely, if not entirely, confined to the mill on the Mitcham side of the river. There is no further record of snuff milling at the Morden mill, and it would seem to have been empty and increasingly derelict until demolished in 1922.[16]

Hillier observed in 1951

> "On the opposite bank to the Grove Mills was a snuff-mill pulled down within the memory of the fibre-works foreman, who in fact dismantled the wheel, an old wooden one, as it was becoming dangerous to the children who played about it. Lying athwart the grassy bank are the snuff-miller's discarded stones, one entire, the other in pieces, and forming, in the manner of the old engravers' imbroglios of skulls, a sort of *memento mori* of water-milling on the Wandle."[17]

The site of the old Morden snuff mill is now owned by the National Trust, the land having been given to the Trust by the Urban District Council of Merton and Morden shortly before it was abolished in the reorganisation of London Government in 1965. The brick retaining walls at the side of the tailrace, and a sill in the bed of the river still survive to mark the approximate position of the wheel, and the complete edge-runner stone Hillier noted lies beneath a tree on the river bank.

Richard Glover II's younger brother John also followed in their father's footsteps, and the two, with their own sons, maintained the family's connections with milling and Mitcham until the middle of the 19th century. Richard junior lived at No. 477 until about 1845, and was in charge of the snuff and tobacco manufactory, holding the mills on leases from the Fry family and their descendants, the Spencers.

Like his father, Richard Glover II was a Mitcham vestryman, and in 1833 served as a churchwarden. Sad to relate, financial difficulties were ahead for the family, and in May 1835 one of the Richard Glovers was declared bankrupt, but since three generations bore the same Christian name, it is not clear which one was involved, or which Richard Glover was the occupant of the Mitcham snuff mill in 1838. [13] Whoever

*Morden Snuff Mill c.1906. By this time the mill was disused.*
*(Photograph reproduced by courtesy of Merton Library Service)*

it was, two years later the bankruptcy remained undischarged. "Richard Glover" was recorded at the mills in 1841,[18] but he seems to have ceased business shortly afterwards, and by the mid-1840s the former snuff mills, with their kiln house, yard and buildings on the north bank of the river were unoccupied and, presumably, disused.[19]

Whereas the retirement of the Glovers from the scene saw the end of snuff milling in the vicinity of Mitcham bridge, the industry was to continue downstream at Ravensbury and Morden Hall for many years. Richard Glover II died in 1858 at the age of 68 and his headstone stands in Mitcham churchyard, marking also the grave of his wife Sarah and their son Richard, who died only three years after his father.

## The Paper Mill

The canal-like watercourse in the Watermeads known today as 'Paper Mill Cut' is clearly marked on the plan produced from a survey of the estate of Henry Hoare conducted in 1827. This accompanied the sale particulars prepared when his freehold and leasehold estate was auctioned in 1828, and also shows a large building, L-shaped in plan, standing at the head of the cut, near the present weir.[1]

This building was the paper mill referred to in the sale particulars and which, with 'Paper Mill Cut', fishponds and various parcels of land now incorporated in the Watermeads, was held by Richard Glover under an 85-year lease which commenced at Midsummer 1778. It has not been possible to find a precise date for the construction of the building, nor for the digging of the cut, which ensured the retention of a substantial volume of water with a working head of some four feet. The amount of work involved in its excavation was considerable, and the expectation of profit obviously substantial. Rather unexpectedly, neither the mill building nor the cut is identifiable on the first edition Ordnance Survey map of 1816, but the scale is such that many smaller details must, of necessity, have been omitted. They are similarly missing from both Bryant's and the Greenwoods' maps of 1823, produced on a much larger scale. Bryant makes the specific claim that his map was surveyed in 1822 and 1823, and comparison with the OS map shows considerable additions. On the cartographical evidence, therefore, Paper Mill Cut as it exists today has to be dated to the period 1824-27 but, as we shall see below, it may have been constructed a decade or so earlier.

The circumstances under which the lease came to be in Henry Hoare's possession are not known, nor the date when the transfer occurred, but the land tax records suggest that his interest in the property commenced around 1795. As the senior partner of Hoare's Bank since 1782, and having known Glover as a neighbour for a number of years, Hoare might well have arranged both for the initial financing of the paper mill, and also working capital, taking the lease as collateral security. Further research, for instance in the archives of Hoare's Bank, might well clarify the situation.

Work by Alan Crocker shows that Richard Glover, in addition to his other milling activities, was manufacturing paper at his mill "at Morden" between 1782 and 1814,[2] and that he employed a variant of the popular Britannia watermark, to be seen, for instance, in the paper used for the Mitcham land tax books for 1795 and 1798. Glover was an established figure in the industry, and at the General Meeting of the Master Paper Makers in 1799 was represented by Thomas Curteis of Carshalton and Charles Ball of Chilworth, both paper makers.

*'Paper Mill Cut' in the Watermeads seen from the south c.1990 (ENM)*

According to Crocker, around 1810-1820 a number of Surrey paper makers producing hand-made paper became bankrupt, but in most instances after a lapse of a year or so the mills re-opened to produce machine-made paper.[3] It seems that about this time changes were also occurring at Morden, with enlargement of the mill and perhaps construction of the cut and the digging of a millpond – the so-called 'Jack Pond' – but much more evidence is needed before one can be sure. It may, however, be significant that in 1814 Richard Glover, "paper maker of Mitcham", insured his paper mill at Morden near Mitcham bridge with the Sun Insurance Company.[4]

According to Crocker, Glover's activity as a paper manufacturer at Morden ceased around 1828 – another significant date, for this was when Henry Hoare died and the remaining portion of the lease of the paper mill and land was sold.[1] Mention of "the paper mill" in the record kept of a perambulation of the bounds of Mitcham in 1833 shows that even if no longer in use for paper making, the building was still standing at that time.[5] In 1834 what seems to have been the mill building was recorded as "empty".[6] Three years later, when the tithe commissioners

*Watermark and countermark traced from paper made by Richard Glover at Morden Mill. Shown about half-size. Reproduced by courtesy of A Crocker.*

were conducting a survey in the parish of Morden, Richard Glover's second son, John, was found to be leasing or renting a garden, "a large building", probably his father's old paper mill, and six acres of meadow now within the Watermeads. The land owner appears in their register as "Mrs Spencer (late Fry)".[7]

It is not known when the old paper mill building was demolished, but it had gone by the time the second edition of the 25 inch OS map was surveyed in 1894. Today its site is a level plot of greensward in the Watermeads at the head of Paper Mill Cut. Here the brickwork of the mill race can still be seen, and the mill tail through which the water held in the cut flows to rejoin the main river.

## The Surrey Iron Railway

Both Hillier and Francis have claimed [1] that for a time early in the 19th century part of the Crown Mill or, more likely, separate buildings at the rear,[2] were workshops in which the horse-drawn trucks, used on the Surrey Iron Railway, were repaired. From 1803 to the early 1840s the railway passed 300 yards to the north of the mill site along what is today called Tramway Path. Corn and coal were two of the main commodities carried, a steady supply of which would have been required either at the mills or the nearby Globe Brewery.

Factories and other customers used their own trucks, which might well have been repaired on their premises. There is no direct evidence of any of the various buildings associated with the Wandle mills being used for this purpose, but the idea is given support by the discovery of large cast-iron wheels, which had been embedded in the sides of the river bank to act as a reinforcement. Several of these wheels were dislodged by the current after heavy rainfall and flooding in January 1936, and were discovered in the bed of the tailrace of the Crown Mill, where they remained visible in the 1940s.

Two of the wheels were salvaged in 1969 by National Trust staff and taken as curios to the snuff mills at Morden Hall. The least damaged, three feet in diameter, unflanged and having nine spokes, was subsequently offered by the Trust to Surrey Archaeological Society on

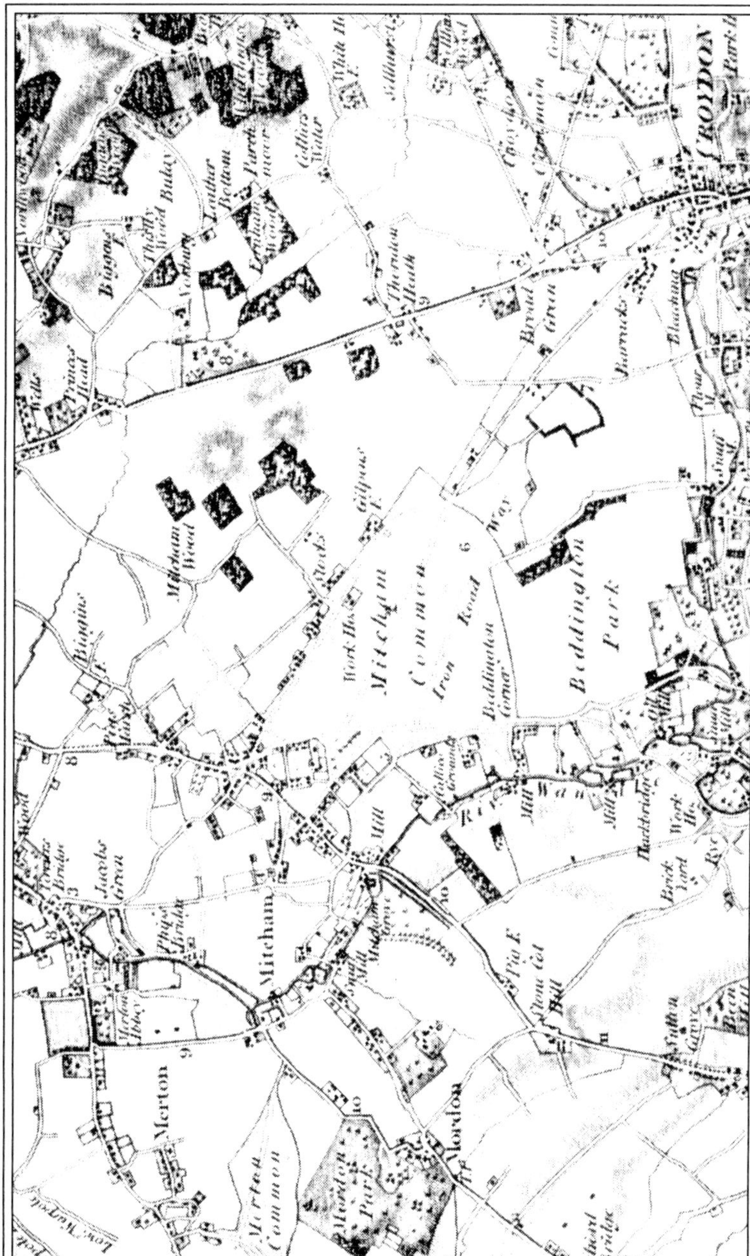


*Detail from 1st edition OS map of 1816, showing 'Iron Road Way', or Surrey Iron Railway*

extended loan, and was transported to the Castle Arch Museum at Guildford in 1972 by the writer. The other is now in the custody of the Wandle Industrial Museum, where it is on display with an iron plate rail, and two stone sleeper pads loaned by Merton Historical Society.

Both wheels are of a type known to have been fitted to trucks used on the railway and it quite possible for them to have come from wagons owned by the Glovers or the brewery and used to transport goods to and from the railhead at Wandsworth Creek.

*Wagon wheel from the Surrey Iron Railway, salvaged from the bed of the Wandle above Mitcham bridge. It is now in Guildford Museum. (ENM 1972)*

## John Glover, Flour Miller (1833-1855)

What the sale particulars of the late Henry Hoare's estate described as "Two capital Water Corn Mills ... With a powerful head of water, well supplied from the River Wandle, working Five Pair of Stone, Four Stories high" were both in the occupation of John Glover. The four-storey millhouse (presumably the fore-runner of the Grove Mill), with its associated buildings, was held on a 91-year lease from Midsummer

1772, and was clearly the successor to that which Richard Glover had taken over from Lionel Gregory in 1774. The other mill was held under a lease for 21 years from Lady-Day 1814, and is shown on the accompanying plan to have been behind and at an angle to the older building, but supplied from the same mill head.[1] The sale of the leasehold property was conducted by Robins, the auctioneer, in the summer of 1828 at Garroway's Coffee House in Cornhill, the lot comprising the two watermills also including a 'Cottage Residence', offices and stabling.[1]

John, Richard Glover's second son, was a flour miller all his life. He seems to have followed his father at the Grove Mill, although in a review of Wandle mills conducted in 1834 Richard and John were recorded jointly as lessees and occupiers of the corn mill, whilst the owners were said, somewhat enigmatically, to be "Crockfords".[2] John Glover first appeared as a miller in his own right in the commercial directories in 1839,[3] and by the 1840s had attained the status of a master miller, employing two men.[4] The Mitcham tithe survey records show him occupying the flour mills, and the miller's house and gardens on the north bank of the river, with land ownership remaining in the hands of the Spencers,[5] and he, his wife and son John are also listed, as might be expected, in the census returns.

Late 19th-century photographs portray the Grove Mill as a long, rectangular building, occupying roughly the same area as the present structure, but of four storeys rather than three. Behind the mill there was a large mill pond, created by a diversion of the Wandle and impounding a considerable volume of water. By 1853 this powered not only the 24 hp wheel of Glover's corn mill, but also another of 20 hp serving Ashby's corn mills. Both, it seems, were housed within the Grove Mill building. Another wheel, of 23 hp and once driving the snuff mill, now served "Mr. Jones's felt mill".[7] The tailrace of the flour mills passed under Grove Mill and discharged below the bridge which gave access to the front and rear of the building, whilst the tail from the felt mill passed round the south of the mill cottages, following the parish boundary and what one therefore assumes to have been the course of the Wandle during the Middle Ages.

John Glover's name last appears in the Post Office directory for 1855, and was replaced in the 1862 edition by that of Joshua Ashby of Brixton. Glover and his family seem to have vacated the miller's house at about the same time. The mid-19th century in fact marks a watershed not only in the story of the Glover family, but also in the history of the mills and the houses so intimately associated with them.

## The Crown and Grove Mills (1850-1900): Felt and Flour

During the late 1840s what had been the Glovers' snuff mill on the Mitcham side of the river was acquired and adapted by Richard Jones, a felt manufacturer. A newcomer to the district, by 1846 Jones and his family had taken up residence at Mitcham House, overlooking the Upper Green.[1] John Edmunds, his manager, had moved into No. 477 with his family between 1846 and 1851,[2] and by 1855 the Mitcham Felt Mills were busily producing boots and jerkins for British troops engaged in the Crimean War.[3] No. 475 London Road, the last of the three houses to be built and the one to be seen facing the road bridge, dates from shortly after 1851, and it is likely it was erected at the behest of Richard Jones, but this has not been confirmed.

Power for the felt mill came from a single great wheel, generating 23 horsepower.[4] Under R R Whitehead Bros Ltd, the firm which had absorbed Jones's business by the early 1860s,[5] the manufacture of felt goods continued for nearly 50 years at the Crown Mill. In 1870 a fire at the 'Wandle Felt Works', as it was commonly known, necessitated rebuilding, but the damage was made good in six weeks, and production was hardly affected. However, since, like the building it replaced, the new mill was not parallel to the wheel, which had survived the fire, special gears had to be cut to transmit the drive to the machinery. The wheel is understood to have remained in working order until the 1960s.[6]

The Ashbys, the new occupiers of the Grove flour mill, were a Quaker family of Irish descent, who became prominent millers in south-eastern London in the 19th century. The business had been founded by John Ashby, who died in the early 1840s, and the smock windmill he erected in 1816 at Brixton Hill still stands.[7] John Robert Ashby was listed in the 1845 directory for Mitcham as a maltster, and six years later the

"Ashby Brothers" appear as "millers, Lower Mitcham".[8] Increasing urbanisation of the Brixton area eventually induced John Ashby's son Joshua to transfer the business to the mills at Lower Mitcham, where the river Wandle offered a reliable source of power for their milling machinery.[9]

The Ashbys' lease of the Grove Mill expired in August 1902 [7] and the 900-year history of flour milling by Mitcham bridge came to an end. A new era was to begin, however, with the arrival in 1903 of fresh tenants, the Patent Horse Hair Co Ltd.[10] At this time horse hair, used very widely for upholstery, was often adulterated by the addition of hogs' hair to reduce the price, and consequently the quality suffered. Concurrently there was emerging a growing public awareness of the need for better hygienic standards in filling materials generally, which were often of questionable cleanliness. To meet the demand for material which had the toughness and resilience of curled horsehair, but lacked its disadvantages, a new synthetic filling was developed by a chemist named Holmes. Recognising the advantages of a vegetable fibre free from animal contaminants, which would not support bacterial or fungal

*The Grove Flour Mill, occupied by the Ashby Brothers until 1902 (Photograph reproduced by courtesy of Merton Library Service)*

growth, he selected fibres like coir and 'Algerian fibre', both possessing good tensile strength and capable of being sterilised and then treated with a synthetic coating. Holmes succeeded in producing an impregnated fibre to which a curl could be imparted, and which provided the tough, resilient and rot-resistant fibre needed for mattresses and furniture.

## Mitcham Hair and Fibre Mills (1903-1955)

William Wright Thompson, one-time managing director of R R Whitehead Brothers Ltd, was well known locally as an outstanding cricketer.[1] He was associated with Holmes in the development of the new filling material (it was Thompson's idea to call it 'Lyxhayr'), which they patented. Lyxhayr was an immediate success when placed on the market, and in 1905 the Patent Horse Hair Company changed its name to Lyxhayr Ltd. Two years later the new firm suffered a temporary setback when another serious fire gutted the Grove Mill. The building was virtually destroyed, but fortunately during rebuilding it was possible for production to be continued in the nearby Crown Mill, then vacant and largely disused since the departure of Whiteheads.[2] By 1907 part of the Crown Mill was used by a Mr Seager for making what one of my informants [3] referred to as "furniture polish", but another,[4] probably more accurately, described as "gin". Seager, a Dutchman, returned to Holland in 1914.

Ashby's former corn mill is visible in various photographs taken around the turn of the century as a large building of three storeys, built of stock brick. The roof was of slate, and projecting from the centre of the top floor was the usual gabled sack hoist. When rebuilt after the fire (by local builder Charles Sayers & Son) the top storey was not renewed, resulting in the two-storeyed building which survives today.[5] The lower part of the walls and the ground plan were retained, but a small extension was added to the west. In 1910 a new wheel, with an output of 100 hp was supplied by A & C Jenner Ltd, engineers of Fair Green, Mitcham. who had installed the replacement machinery after the fire.[6] Hillier observed that the new wheel was all metal, cast in the traditional manner, but somewhat unusual in his view in that it had a width greater than its diameter.[7]

*The Crown Mill seen from the Watermeads, from a drawing by Dewey-Bates,* The English Illustrated Magazine *1888-1889*

*Morden Mill, c.1910. (Photograph, believed to have been taken by Tom Francis, reproduced by courtesy of Merton Library Service)*

By 1910 the demand for Lyxhayr had increased to such an extent that a lease of the Crown Mill was taken on by Lyxhayr Ltd.[8] Fresh capital was introduced, and the firm reformed under the name of Lyxhayr Manufacturers Ltd with W A Dickinson as managing director. Dickinson was an active participant in the move towards better hygienic standards in the furniture and bedding industry, and was one of the founders of the Bedding Federation. He was also instrumental in securing the passage of the Rag Flock Act 1911, the first legislative attempt to raise the hygienic quality of filling materials. Locally, Dickinson was a staunch supporter of residents seeking to improve the quality of the Wandle, and to conserve riverside amenities. He was one of the original members of the River Wandle Open Spaces Committee, and played a prominent part in the effort which resulted in ownership of the Watermeads and Happy Valley being transferred to the National Trust.[8]

The history of the next 40 years at the Grove and Crown Mills has been dealt with by E B Hedger,[6] who joined the firm of Lyxhayr Ltd as an office boy in 1915, and spent the whole of his working life in the business, retiring as managing director of the Mitcham Hair and Fibre Mills Ltd. During his time the variety of products and the volume of output increased phenomenally, and the firm achieved a worldwide reputation. Two World Wars boosted production to meet the needs of the armed services and in particular the hospitals. A direct hit on the Grove Mill during an air raid in November 1940 failed to halt production, and the power crisis of 1947 was overcome by recourse to the waterwheel, still able to fulfil its original function of keeping machinery in motion.

The freehold of the mills, already held on a long lease, had been purchased by the Mitcham Fibre Mills Ltd from Sir Frederick Fowke in 1919.[8] During the summer of 1940, at the height of the Battle of Britain, Alfred Smith, the steward of the manor of Reigate, saw fit to write to Hedger, then company secretary and manager of the mills, drawing attention to the payment of the quit rent of £1 due annually since the change of ownership of Crown Mill 20 years previously. He suggested the situation might be resolved by extinguishment of the "manorial incidents" by voluntary agreement under the provisions of the Law of Property Act 1922. The steward's timing could have been better chosen, for Hedger was then somewhat preoccupied with the difficulties of maintaining production under war conditions. Understandably he was not inclined to go into the matter at the time, and the question of back rent due to the lord of the manor seems to have been left unresolved.

It was with expressions of confidence in the future of Mitcham Hair and Fibre Mills that Hedger concluded his review of its first half century in 1953. Events were to prove him wrong, however, for within a few years of the 50th anniversary of its foundation, Mitcham Hair and Fibres Mills Ltd was bought out by a firm in High Wycombe. At the same time the Grove Mill was sold to R F White and Co Ltd, a firm of toilet soap manufacturers and perfumiers whose products were marketed under the brand name 'Jean Sorelle', and to whom part of the premises had been leased in 1930.[8]

## The Recent Past: 1960–

As we have seen, the pond behind the Grove Mill was filled in during the course of flood prevention work by Surrey County Council in the early 1960s. A flow of water was maintained beneath the mill by an 18-inch pipe laid from near the new weir in the Watermeads and discharging into the tailrace in front of the building, but by this time the great waterwheel was completely obsolete, and it was removed to release more floor space. The building itself is, nevertheless, recognised as being of some interest, and is included in the local list of buildings of historical or architectural significance held by the London Borough of Merton. When the premises were visited by the writer in July 1966, one of the company directors – a Mr Gauntlet, who had worked on the premises for 35 years – confirmed that all traces of the old mill machinery had then gone from inside the building. Although completely dry, the inlet flume through which water from the mill pond had once been directed beneath the building could still be seen at the rear as late as 2004.

The Crown Mill, erected by Whiteheads after Glover's former snuff mill had been burned down in 1870, was acquired by C S Walker (Sacks) Ltd and the Associated Jute Co. Ltd in 1959. The massive 18-foot diameter wheel, 10 feet broad, and giving an impression of great power, was still in working order at this time and was actually put to use experimentally in 1962 or 1963 by the Walkers, driving machinery to beat the dust out of used sacks which were being renovated for resale. In 1964 the Crown Mill was destroyed by fire, and was not rebuilt. The wheel, which had been positioned between the Crown Mill and the adjoining Grove Mill, was rendered useless and was dismantled. All trace of it sadly vanished, together with the mill gates and the tumbling-bay, slight changes in the ground level and the paving of the works yard being the only indications of where the wheel might have been.

In February 1975 the local press reported that R F White & Co Ltd, by this time owned by the Dunbee Combex Marx Group, was closing down the Mitcham works and moving to Peterborough. The fine quality soaps produced by White and Company were exported all over the world, and one of their specialities was the manufacture of soap bars for children, moulded into likenesses of television and Disney characters. For the 70 or so workers, most of them local women and many part-time, the loss of employment by White and Co. was a severe blow.

'For Sale' boards were soon in evidence, and two years later the Grove Mill was purchased by Footman and Co Ltd, a firm founded in 1948 by Arthur Footman and two assistants to serve the growing needs of post-war chiropody healthcare. Dedicated solely to the manufacture and marketing of chiropody supplies and podological equipment, by 1993 the firm was the largest organisation of its kind in the United Kingdom, and had developed an export trade with over 40 countries. The history of the building and the site it occupied was not overlooked by the owners, and their trade literature made mention of the possibility that here, or close by, a watermill was working over 900 years ago.

A decade later the situation had changed again, Footman & Co Ltd had left, and the Grove Mill, a locally listed building, awaited conversion into apartments by Bewley Homes plc.

# Chapter 6

## 'WANDLE GROVE' OR 'WANDLE HOUSE', AND THE BROOKFIELDS ESTATE

Through the medium of a large number of deeds surviving from the Tudor period onwards it is possible to follow in some detail the history of the land on which the houses in Riverside Drive and Brookfields Avenue were built in the 1930s. With a little less assurance the story of this corner of Lower Mitcham can be traced back to the 14th century and the de la Mare family, and before them the Anglo-Norman de Whitfords. As we have already noted, in 1362 William Mareys presented to the Church his estate in "Wykford", consisting of a substantial house, with "gardens, crofts, meadows, pastures, woods, trees, hedges, hays and ditches ...", two watermills and an adjoining " piece of moor", or marshy ground on the banks of the river. The property extended from just south of the Cricket Green to as far as Green Wrythe Lane, and for nearly 200 years what became known as 'Maresland' producd an income for Merton priory.

In 1544, following the dissolution of the priory, a substantial portion of the estate came into the possession of Robert Wilford, a London merchant, and thereafter tenure passed through various hands but, remarkably, although subdivided, sold, leased and sub-leased over the centuries, its constituent parts can still be identified, albeit tentatively, and the old boundaries indicated on a modern map. By the early 17th century the Brookfields estate seems to have been part of the 30 acres of marsh ground held of the manor of Reigate by George Smythe. In 1645, what appears to have been the same parcel of "marsh ground", by then "enclosed with pales", was included in the property at Mitcham offered as security for a loan by Thomas Smythe, George's brother.

The impressive Wandle Grove or, to give it its modern name, Wandle House, No. 10 Riverside Drive, Mitcham, was first listed as a building of architectural and historic importance in 1954, with the comment "Grade II c. 1780. The house bears a considerable resemblance to 'The Wick' on Richmond Hill, which is listed Grade I."[1] Nairn and Pevsner,[2] commenting that "Robert Mylne, in reviving Palladian detail, achieved a new delicacy of touch", were of the view that The Wick, built in 1775, is "one of his most handsome villas". They also expressed the opinion that Wandle House, built as was then fashionable in yellow stock bricks, with its ground floor windows under blank arches, and an intermittently balustraded parapet, is so similar that it is probably his also. We have nothing to support this assumption, and the identity of Mylne's client at Mitcham (if, indeed, he was the architect) is not known. One feels bound to remark on the similarity between much of the detailing of Wandle House and that of Mitcham Grove, which stood on the opposite side of the main road and had been the property of the London banker, Henry Hoare, since 1786. Did he, perhaps, finance the building of the new house, having leased the land from the Frye family, the freeholders, and might not the appearance of Mitcham Grove, which had been substantially 'modernised' in the 18th century, have influenced the design of Wandle House?

*Wandle House, 10 Riverside Drive, Mitcham*
*Photographed in 1961 by Surrey County Council Planning Department.*
*Copyright Surrey County Council (R18B). Reproduced by permission.*

In 1768 two 'closes' of land. which can be identified by subsequent deeds as providing the sites on which Wandle House and the later Brookfields housing estate were built, were part of a property sold to Rowland Frye of Wallington.[3] There is mention of "a messuage, garden and yard adjoining", and the vendor was William Myers, whose ancestors, the Smythes, had owned the property since the end of the 16th century. The first hint of a new house likely to have been Wandle House (guided by its assessment of £70 p.a. and its position in the records) is in the land tax book for 1795,[4] It is also in Edwards's map produced in about 1801.[5] The freeholder at this time was William Fry(e), who owned other property in Lower Mitcham and Carshalton, and the occupier of the new house was Thomas Hinchcliffe who, if the above supposition is correct, was Hoare's tenant or a sub-lessee. Hinchcliffe, about whom very little is known by the writer at the present time, died in 1802 and was buried at Mitcham. The vestry minutes for 1805 mention his widow, Elizabeth Hinchcliffe, as customarily occupying part of the gallery across the north aisle of the parish church, and William Monson recalled from his schooldays at the Revd Roberts's Academy in Mitcham the Hinchcliffe family, and particularly one of the daughters, "a pretty lively girl". She was Mrs Roberts's "greatest friend", and sometimes accompanied the boys on their walks. Another frequent visitor to the Hinchliffe household was the Abbé Le Taillot, an emigré who taught French and geography at Roberts's Academy. Wandle Grove (as the house now seems to have been known) appears to have remained Elizabeth Hinchcliffe's home until around 1821, after which it stood vacant for about a year.[4] For six years thereafter the tax books refer to the house as "late Hinchcliffe", without naming the occupier.

The phenomenon of a large house standing empty for several years was not at all uncommon in Mitcham at this time, and can perhaps be seen as a consequence of the economic depression following the end of the Napoleonic Wars. It does appear, however, that for a period during the mid-1820s, Wandle Grove was used by Henry Hoare, for the Greenwoods, who described it as a "spacious mansion", stated that it was "the property of Henry Hoare, banker, temporarily occupied by members of Mr. Hoare's family".[6] This cannot be confirmed from the land tax records which, as we have seen, from 1823 to 1828 merely describe the house and land as "late Hinchcliffe". The truth probably is that at this time Henry Hoare, a widower in his mid-70s, took Wandle Grove to accommodate six of his many grandchildren who, with their governess and nurses, came to live with him at Mitcham Grove in 1819 following the death of their parents. Great as his attachment undoubtedly was to his family, there must have been times when Mitcham Grove, despite its size, could not afford the old gentleman the peace and privacy he needed, and the use of Wandle Grove for the growing children would seem to have been an ideal solution.

On Henry Hoare's death in 1828, his large estate of freehold and leasehold property was sold by auction and the family's connection with Mitcham Grove was severed. Wandle Grove was described in the sale particulars as leasehold, and

> " ... placed on a beautiful Lawn, surrounded by fine thriving Plantations and Evergreens, Shrubbery, Cedar and stately Timber Trees, delightful Walks by the Side of the River Wandle."[7]

The house was approached from the turnpike road by a "handsome Carriage Drive". A "bowed Drawing Room" with marble chimney piece was the principal room on the slightly raised ground floor, entered from the inner hall, off which there were also a dining parlour and "neat Library", as well as the usual domestic offices comprising kitchen, housekeeper's room, china closet, scullery etc. On the first floor, reached by a "Commodious staircase", were four "excellent Bed Chambers", a dressing room and water closet. All the rooms were papered. The upper floor contained three further bedrooms and the housemaids' closet, whilst in the basement were the butler's pantry, dairy, larder, "knife hole" and the wine and beer cellars.[7]

Outside were to be found the usual accompaniments of the typical small farmstead supporting a house of this character, including piggery, mushroom shed, cow house, a four-stall stable with loft over, and a coach house. The "Excellent Kitchen Garden" was said to be well-stocked, cropped and planted with choice fruit trees, and there was also a hot house.[7]

Wandle Grove, with its 12 acres of gardens and meadowland, was sold for £2,440. The following year the tax assessors once again recorded the house as 'empty', but it was not long before the new owners arrived, and the house became the home of John Wilson and his wife Mary.[8] Wilson, a farmer's son from Nottinghamshire, had completed his apprenticeship with a Newark linen-draper when, at the age of 19, he made his way to London in 1793 and found employment with Jasper Capper of Gracechurch Street. Within a short time he was offered a partnership, and in 1802 opened his own shop at Covent Garden. Two years later he married Mary Jones, the daughter of Martha Jones, the widowed Vauxhall potter who with John Watts and John Doulton was to found the famous Lambeth potteries bearing the latter's name. John and Mary Wilson had four sons and two daughters. The family business prospered and William, the eldest son, was the first of the three Wilson boys who were ultimately to join their father in the new shop he had established in fashionable Old Bond Street. By 1829 John Wilson's health was failing. The owner of the farm they leased at Greenhill, Hampstead, had asked the Wilsons to leave, and, after a search in Hammersmith and Wandsworth they found Wandle Grove, delightfully situated in a wooded riverside setting, and with its own small farm. It was here that John Wilson spent his last years, and where he died in February 1835 at the age of 60. His tomb is in Mitcham churchyard, beneath the east window of the chancel. Anne, his eldest daughter, was an accomplished watercolour artist, and whilst staying with her parents she painted a number of charming views of the house and grounds. In 1838 Mary was obliged to leave Wandle Grove, which was to be sold, and moved to Chester Terrace. She died the same year, after a short visit to Paris, and was buried beside her husband at Mitcham.[9]

Later that year, when Crawter and Nash were surveying Mitcham for the Poor Law Commissioners, Brookfields Cottage, a villa built nearby in the grounds of Wandle Grove, was occupied by the curate of Mitcham, the Revd Herbert Randolph, and his wife Martha, whom he married the previous September. She, sadly, died in January 1839 very shortly after the birth of their daughter Martha Jane. Randolph left Mitcham later that year, having secured an appointment as vicar at Abbotsley, Hunts.[10]

The Wilson family connection with Mitcham was not severed with the mother's death, however, for in about 1839 William Wilson and his wife Emily moved into Brookfield Cottage, where they lived with their little son Arthur throughout the 1840s. Brookfield(s) Cottage, a leasehold property, had also featured in the sale of Henry Hoare's estate. The accommodation was quite modest, comprising a "Dining Parlour", walls papered and "with a veined marble chimneypiece," a breakfast parlour and usual offices, whilst on the first floor were four bedrooms with closets etc. Outside, there was a "Capital Kitchen Garden and Pleasure Ground." In 1828 the whole had been let to a Mrs Beecher "aged Eighty-six, for her Life" at a rental of 19 guineas per annum.[7]

William Wilson and his brother Henry managed the family shop in town until they died in the 1850s, whilst John, the youngest brother, was the proprietor of the Globe Brewery at Mitcham. In 1847, accompanied by John, the two sisters, neither of whom married, undertook a nine-month tour of Europe, returning to Brookfields Cottage in October. Mary's dairy of the journey formed the basis for a book, copiously illustrated with Anne's watercolours, from which much of the foregoing information has been extracted.[9]

The Mitcham tithe register confirms William Wilson as the occupier of Brookfields Cottage, and Richard Spencer as the landowner. The cottage, the appearance of which Anne captured in a watercolour dated 1836, can be seen to the north of Wandle Grove in the Ordnance Survey maps of 1867 and 1895. The last occupant of note appears to have been S P Torr(e), father of the author C Torre, who is listed as resident at Brookfields Cottage in Green's *South London Directory* published in 1869. The name was perpetuated in Brookfields Farm, which seems to have survived the cottage, and then much later by Brookfields Avenue which, with Riverside Drive, serves the 1930s housing estate which covers the meadows and gardens of Wandle Grove. William Wilson is remembered in the parish church as the donor of two silver cups, bearing the inscription "The Gift of William Wilson Esq., of Wandle Grove, Mitcham, 1848".[11]

In 1841 Wandle Grove was occupied by a William Loraine, described as of independent means in the census of that year, his wife and family of nine children. The household included three other adults, presumably relatives, and five servants living-in. Six years later Wandle Grove, with its lodge, gardens and shrubberies, and the meadows which extended to the banks of the Wandle – in all totalling a little over 11 acres – was in the tenure of Henry Hopkins, presumably on a lease from Richard Spencer, the owner.[12] One is obliged to admit that nothing is known of these two families, and much the same has to be said for the majority of their successors.[13] William Beebe, a hide and skin broker, and his wife were recorded as residents at Wandle Grove in 1851.[14] They evidently enjoyed a position in the local social hierachy in keeping with the rather fine house they occupied, and Beebe's name appears in the section of the local Mitcham directories devoted to 'The Gentry', where he was deferentially afforded the style of 'esquire'.[15]

***Opposite:*** *Brookfields Cottage, Mitcham, May 1840, viewed from the west. Wandle Grove is just visible to the right. Copy of a watercolour by Anne Wilson, published in* A European Journal: Two Sisters Abroad in 1847*, by Mary Wilson (1987). Attempts to trace the copyright owner have proved unsuccessful.*

So the story of Wandle Grove continues throughout the second half of the 19th century, with quite frequent changes of occupancy. Green's Directory records a Frederick John Duckworth there in 1869 [16] and the following year, when his address was given as Brabant Court, Philpot Lane, London, he was granted a 14½ years lease of the property by a Robert Green and others of Milford House, Derbyshire.[17] Duckworth thereafter disappears from the local scene, and within a year or so we find references to Mr and Mrs William Stair Mitchell being in residence.[18] Mrs Mitchell is mentioned in the Revd Wilson's pastoral letters, and like many middle-class ladies of her time was obviously active in church affairs. In 1888, following the death of her husband, Mrs Mitchell presented Mitcham parish church with a new pulpit in his memory.

At the turn of the century Wandle Grove was occupied by a Mr Jenner, a trotting enthusiast who is said to have indulged his love of the sport by laying out a track encircling the lawns of nearby Mitcham Grove,

*Wandle House, 10 Riverside Drive, Mitcham*
*Photographed in 1961 by Surrey County Council Planning Department.*
*Copyright Surrey County Council (R18A). Reproduced by permission.*

which had been demolished 50 years previously.[19] The estate was at this time being sold off in lots, and in 1901 the old walled garden of Mitcham Grove and some of the outbuildings surviving from Henry Hoare's time were taken over by the silent film company of Cricks and Sharp. Comic shorts were a speciality, and many of the sequences were filmed 'on location' on (or in) the Wandle nearby. Extras for the crowd scenes were often recruited locally, the inducements (if any were needed) ranging from the price of a couple of pints of beer to as much as half-a-crown a day. Stars had scarcely begun to emerge in those early days, and Jenner's daughter would sometimes play the heroine, strapped to the rails of the local branch line, or locked by the villain in the old snuff mill in Morden Meadow to await 'a fate worse than death'.

After being occupied by a Major Wyndham Quinn for a few years at the beginning of the 20th century, Wandle Grove (by this time the house seems to have been renamed 'Wandle House') was taken over by Mrs Collier, who purchased the freehold from Sir Frederick Fowke in 1919. She was the sister of Sir Cato Worsfold of Hall Place, Church Road, Mitcham, and a member of a family associated with the village since the early 18th century. Sir Frederick also owned Deeds Mill, the Grove and Crown Mills, the river bed between Willow Lane and Mitcham Bridge, the Watermeads and land as far south as the 'Hilly Fields' (now known as Poulter Park). He had been disposing of the estate gradually for several years, selling the Watermeads to the National Trust in 1913, and the Grove and Crown Mills to the Mitcham Hair and Fibre Mills Ltd in 1919.[20]

The part of the estate known as Grove Farm, on which watercress had been grown for many years, was taken over by E James and Son in 1920. Each year the farm produced hundreds of tons of watercress for the London area, marketed under the trade name of 'Vitacress'. Water had been drawn originally from the Wandle but, very conscious of the increasing danger of pollution, which had been demonstrated by an outbreak of typhoid in Croydon in the 1930s, the proprietors sank a 300-foot bore into the chalk from which water of great bacteriological purity was drawn by pump. E James and Son were the last commercial growers of watercress in Mitcham, and ceased production in 1960, moving to Hampshire.[21]

In 1937 the executors of the Collier estate disposed of Wandle House to Howard (Mitcham) Ltd, in whose hands the old house remained until 1968. Howard's business was property development, and within a short time of completing acquisition their proposals for the new Brookfields Estate, covering the five acres of meadowland once belonging to Wandle Grove, had received the approval of Mitcham Borough Council, and building works commenced.

*Typical 1930s' housing in Brookfields Avenue (ENM 1970)*

The development brought to an end the extensive Brookfields Nurseries of J N Cheshire, which had supplied the garden needs of the new housing estates then spreading across the fields of Mitcham and Morden during the phenomenal suburban expansion that marked the late 1920s and 1930s. Howard's proposals also brought them into conflict with E James and Son over the operation of a sluice gate on a mill leet running from an old calico printing works in Willow Lane.[20] This watercourse flowed through the grounds of Wandle House after traversing the James's watercress beds, and discharged into a backwater of the Wandle which had once formed part of the ornamental waters surrounding Henry

*Advertisement from the official guide to Mitcham published in 1937*

Hoare's house. The stream was visible until the mid-1960s in a culvert at the rear of 62-74 Riverside Drive, before disappearing into a surface water sewer. It re-appeared in the grounds of Locomotors Ltd on the opposite side of the London Road, but was finally banished underground during the building of the London Borough of Merton's 'Watermeads' housing estate in the 1970s. Development of the Brookfields housing estate was halted by the outbreak of war in 1939, but was completed by Mitcham Corporation in the late 1940s. In compliance with post-war policy, the new units were not let or sold on the open market, but allocated to nominees selected from the Council's housing list in accordance with a points system.

Howard (Mitcham) Ltd expanded in the post-war years into a large organisation undertaking both contract work and private developments, and employing over 500 people. As the company grew the need for improved accommodation became more pressing and, in 1966, following demolition of early Victorian extensions to Wandle House, the original building was adapted to form part of a new head office

*Wandle House, 10 Riverside Drive, following the adaptation of 1966 (ENM)*

building. It was apparent that alterations to the house in about 1848 had been responsible for the removal of the original staircase and some of the contemporary joinery. Eighteenth-century panelled doors and doorcases, window jambs and soffit linings survived, however, and lent grace to several of the rooms. The Victorian staircase was in the extension which had to be removed to make way for the new office block. Two hundred years separate the constituent parts of the present building, and although they were in such contrastingly different styles, the marriage is not an unhappy one. The 18th-century house is rightly given pride of place, and is the first to meet the eye of the visitor. The extension is sympathetic in mass and form, and being linked to the old with a careful use of glass, avoids too harsh a contrast. The new offices were officially opened in April 1966, the directors of M Howard (Mitcham) Ltd holding a cocktail party for the architects, representatives of local organisations and others connected with the building industry.[22]

Within less than three years, Howard (Mitcham) Ltd had been obliged for financial reasons to cease trading and Wandle House had been sold, the new owners being L Mince and Son. The new tenants, Coppas International (UK) Ltd, had been founded in 1957 to provide a specialist consultant service in systems, automation and operation for the oil, petrochemical and process industries. The company expanded rapidly at a time when increasing developments in the Third World were creating a shortage of skilled personnel to run and maintain complex processing installations, as a result of which Britain began to emerge as a leading exporter of technical skills. Wandle House became the company's London headquarters, linked to offices in Aberdeen, Bristol, Dublin, Houston, Toronto and Benghazi. By the early 1980s Coppas International could pride itself on its unique ability to train staff, operate and maintain a refinery or process plant from scratch. Through its operations in over 60 countries it had gained a world-wide reputation as a supplier of sophisticated technical and management services. Seeing its role as one of service and not competition, the company was deservedly proud of the contribution it was making to a new British enterprise which it saw as being of great significance for the future.[23] By May 1985 Coppas International had moved away and in 2005 Wandle House is occupied by Ian Williams Building and Property.

*The former Surrey Brewery building*
*Photographed in 1958 by Surrey County Council Planning Department.*
*Copyright Surrey County Council. Reproduced by permission.*

# Chapter 7

## THE SURREY BREWERY

In the late 1950s widening of the London Road south of Mitcham Station to form a dual carriageway unfortunately necessitated the demolition of a fine group of late 18th- and early 19th-century brick and weatherboard buildings which had survived to form a link with a rural Mitcham and a local industry which is now passing beyond living memory.

Nearest to the station was a pair of semi-detached 'two up and two down' stock-brick cottages with slate roofs. Dating from the early part of Victoria's reign, they were erected in a style which, until recently, was common throughout Mitcham. Lacking modern amenities (a ground floor back addition contained the kitchen/scullery and, entered from outside, the water closet) and in any case standing unacceptably beyond the road widening line established by the highway engineers since before the 1939/45 war, it was obvious they would not be retained.

To the immediate south of the cottages was the factory of Lactagol Ltd, manufacturers of a patent food which a large sign at the works gate proclaimed was needed by "expectant and nursing mothers". Here, in buildings dating back a century or more, had been the 'Mitcham Brewery' run by Attlees, and after them Thunder and Little, famous in the neighbourhood for their Mitcham Ales.[1] The land upon which the brewery stood featured in a sale of 1770 when Crown Field, a six-acre enclosure partially fronting the turnpike road to Sutton, was sold by William Myers to Rowland Frye for £400.[2] The first topographical writer to mention the brewery was Edwards,[3] towards the close of the 18th century, when the premises were occupied by William Hughes, in whose hands the business remained until 1805.[4]

Research by Peter McGow into the records of the Hand in Hand insurance company have disclosed that the brewery was already in existence in January 1767, when the premises were insured by Edward Bond and Thomas Butt.[5] The policy was renewed in January 1774, by which time John Chesterman, the miller, had replaced Butt as a partner.[6] Following Bond's death in 1775, his widow Mary assigned her share in the brewery to William Hughes "of Mitcham, Brewer" in 1776.[7] Evidence of considerable enlargement of the brewery between 1774 and 1781 is provided by an increase in valuation for insurance purposes from £350 to £800.[8] John Chesterman's partnership with Hughes ceased with his death in 1784, and passed to his executors,[9] from whom it was purchased in 1800 by Hughes.[10]

In Hughes's hands the brewery was further enlarged, the valuation being raised to £1450.[11] Coal was available in quantity once the Surrey Iron Railway was opened in 1803, and the two events are probably linked. Hughes remained the sole owner of the brewery until his death in 1805.[12] "William Hughes, brewer, late of this parish" was buried in Mitcham churchyard, where his brick and sandstone altar tomb can still be seen. Here he was joined by his wife Hannah, who died in 1826, aged 83.

The head lease was still in the hands of Mr Hughes's executors when a map of Henry Hoare's Mitcham Grove estate was prepared in 1812,[13] and what would appear to have been a sub-lease of the 'Globe Brewery' was auctioned in 1817.[14] Bull and Peck, the only brewers having an entry in the Mitcham section of a commercial directory of 1824/5,[15] were presumably successors to a man called Marker Gaze, who had held the lease since Hughes's death, but was declared bankrupt in 1817.[16]

*Mitcham Brewery delivery cart, probably 1920s*
*(reproduced by courtesy of Merton Library Service)*

Nothing more can be told of the history of the Globe Brewery until 1841, when the resident brewer and maltster was Thomas Edwards.[17] Four years later the proprietor was John Wilson of Wandle Grove,[18] and in 1846 we find the "Brewhouse, yard and buildings" owned (or leased) by John Birkett and occupied by Mr I C Dear, assignee of Wilson.[19]

By 1853 the name had changed to the 'Wandle Grove Brewery',[20] and 14 years later it was 'The Surrey Brewery'.[21] The changes were almost certainly instigated by new owners, each proprietor seeking to project a fresh image (and a new, improved product?) to influence and attract the drinking public. The name 'Surrey Brewery' endured for well over half a century, for it was certainly current until shortly before the outbreak of the 1914/18 War.

Since the immediate pre-war period water for the brewing process had been obtained from a sub-artesian well, driven 187 feet through the Wandle gravels and the London Clay, and a further 164 feet into the underlying chalk. The water level stood at 38 feet above Ordnance

*In the background are the last buildings of the brewery to survive (ENM 1975)*

datum, or 30 feet below ground level, and had to be raised to the brewery cisterns with pumps. Although chemically hard, the water was of excellent bacteriological purity, and the well was capable of supplying 2,000 gallons per hour. As to the quality of the beer, the records are unfortunately silent.[22]

The brewery house, the residence of brewer Robert Gilbertson in 1851,[23] and many others before and after, is likely to have been the original late 18th-century house occupied by Hughes. Known as 'The Beeches', big and rambling, weatherboarded and multi-gabled, by the late 1950s it was in a dilapidated condition, no doubt having suffered from blast and neglect of maintenance during the war. In the inter-war years the house had been used as a little private preparatory school - the 'Ravensbury School' – but this had closed by the outbreak of war in 1939.

Although the house had been recognised as of historical and architectural interest, and was awarded a Grade III listing, it was pulled down in 1959, only the magnificent copper beech tree which had stood in the back garden being retained. Sadly, disease finally took hold, and the tree was felled as a safety measure in 1975. The name 'The Beeches' was tranferred to the block of maisonettes erected on the site by Mitcham Borough Council. These, too, seemed to have been 'jinxed' and, although so newly built, were soon looking shabby through neglect and vandalism. One particular target of the wreckers was an attractive panel of slate cladding on the lower part of the front elevation, which was gradually loosened and detached. The slate has now been removed and replaced with colour-washed rendering.

The old brewery buildings, derelict and also vandalised, survived for some 20 years after Lactagol's departure. In part they were used for a time by Shead Brothers, a potato packing and wholesaling firm, but they too were demolished by the end of the 20th century, and the yard was used for vehicle storage by Funnells of Sutton, the removal contractors.

# APPENDIX I

Extracts from

*"50 Years at Grove Mills Mitcham. - The Story of Lyxhayr and Service to the Bedding and Upholstery Trades by Mitcham Hair and Fibres Mills Ltd."*

(Written by Mr E B Hedger, Managing Director in 1953, and transcribed in 1967)

" ... less than 10 miles from the heart of London the Wandle runs through Grove Mills. Altogether it is only 9 miles long, it falls no fewer than one hundred and twenty four feet over this short course, an average of fourteen feet to the mile ... In 1086, at the time of the Domesday Survey, there were at least thirteen corn mills on the Wandle.

"Many centuries later a corn mill still operated where Grove Mills stand today. ... it is reputed that felt was manufactured at Grove Mills in 1855 for the boots and jerkins of British Troops engaged in the Crimean War.

" ... Water was expensive for industrial purposes in 1903 and power quite an item, but at Mitcham thanks to the Wandle, it was already 'laid on' for both purposes. Here was an abundance of water for boiling, cleansing, sterilisation, and sufficient power to drive two water wheels each with a capacity of 100 h.p..

"'Lyxhayr' was first manufactured in 1903 by a company called 'The Patent Horse Hair Co. Ltd.' The product was and, of course, still is a unique curled fibre of vegetable origin for many upholstery filling purposes. It was originated by a Mr. Holmes, a chemist, and the process was patented. Also associated with the venture was an important local man, a Mr. W. W. Thompson", ["at one time the owner or manager of the felt factory in the Crown Mill" – Mr Hedger, in a letter to *The Advertiser* 22. 9. 1949] "better known for his connection with the Surrey County Cricket Club. Mr. Thompson coined the trade name 'Lyxhayr', its significance being obvious beneath the disguised spelling.

"Mr. Holmes realised the advantages to be gained by using a vegetable fibre free from animal fat or any matter on which life or germs could subsist. He selected a vegetable fibre of great strength and his process of manufacture expelled the woody matter or tissue in the fibre, refilling the cylinder or elongated tube of the fibre thus emptied with a chemically prepared composition. The material was sterilised, then dyed, and in the last or sealing vat it received a special solution which sealed the pores of the fibre. In its changed condition it became impervious to damp and innocuous as a disease generator.

"There were however several stages to go before Lyxhayr reached its final or marketable stage. The treated fibres were carded and spun into a rope form to impart a curl. The 'ropes' were afterwards untwisted and carded resulting in a hygienic resilient material ideal as a filling for mattresses and furniture.

"Basically the process of manufacture remains the same now as in 1903 although naturally there have been changes in detail and every mechanical device brought to bear to save manual labour.

"The first Lyxhayr 'rope' to be made was recently found in a damp cellar and it is interesting to see that the material still fully retains its curl and that the tensile strength of the fibres remained unimpaired.

"In 1903 no ready-made machinery existed for the manufacture of Lyxhayr and the process had to be improvised. For example, curling the fibre into 'ropes' was, in the experimental stages, undertaken with a domestic type spinning wheel. Some of the necessary machinery was developed by the firm itself. Lyxhayr enjoyed considerable success almost from the first because there was a demand for something better than the then current brand of curled hair. In 1903 horse hair was often adulterated with hog hair to reduce the price and the quality consequently suffered. Lyxhayr had all the advantages of the best curled horse hair besides important qualities of its own. It was used extensively in tropical climates because it was proof against insect attack, even of the White Ant.

"In 1905 the Company changed its name to Lyxhayr Ltd., and by 1907 had made sufficient progress to make new capital necessary and this was provided by Mr. W. A. Dickinson who became Managing Director of the Company.

"Besides expanding Lyxhayr Ltd. very considerably, Mr. Dickinson made his presence felt throughout the industry. For one thing, he was keenly interested in the movement to improve the hygienic standards of those days. As a matter of fact, only since the last war has anything like a proper standard been made compulsory but in 1906 public consciousness had begun to stir in this matter. Before 1911 there was nothing to stop manufacturers from filling mattresses and furniture with most unhygienic materals and so the fillings were often of very questionable origin. Mr. Dickinson was one of those who helped to secure the passing of the Rag Flock Act, 1911, the first attempt to regulate the worst abuses.

"Preserving the amenities of the Wandle was another of Mr. Dickinson's interests and he invariably took up the fight against any threat to the river." [Mr Hedger, in his letter to *The Advertiser* 22. 9. 1949, said Mr. Dickinson was one of the original members of the Watermeads Committee, and had taken an active part in the handing over of the Watermeads and Happy Valley to the National Trust.] "The following year saw the formation of the Bedding Federation, a body of manufacturers and suppliers of materials which has always worked to improve standards of quality and hygiene. Mr. Dickinson helped in the formation of the Federation.

"It may be mentioned here that Lyxhayr was in advance of its time in that it set a standard of cleanliness long before legislation made this compulsory, and when the law did step in no changes in the manufacturing process of Lyxhayr were necessary.

"A big demand for Lyxhayr came from hospitals, especially mental hospitals and infirmaries making up their own bedding. Many old testimonials exist showing how well regarded Lyxhayr was even in those early days. Today, under the new conditions imposed by the National Health Acts, the connection is even stronger.

"In 1907 Lyxhayr Ltd. sustained a serious fire but even this could not upset the Company's steady progress. By 1910 the demands for Lxyhayr had so increased that it became necessary to take over the adjoining Crown Mill, [shown on the 1910 OS map as 'disused'] additional capital was introduced and Lyxhayr Manufacturers Ltd. was formed with Mr. W. A. Dickinson as Managing Director.

"From 1914 until 1918 the entire output had to be devoted to war purposes. being used largely for hospital mattresses needed to accommodate the hundreds of thousands of battle casualties. Many shipments were also sent abroad for use by allied governments.

"During the early years consignments of Lyxhayr were delivered to London bedding manufacturers at a smart pace by paired horse vans. On several occasions drivers incurred the indignation of passers-by and active intervention by the police for their supposed cruelty to the horses. The bulky loads looked far too heavy for two horses, but the material being so light really imposed no strain on the animals.

"In 1915, one E. B. Hedger, a native of Mitcham, joined the firm as an office boy ... The whole of his business life has been spent on the banks of the Wandle, although he had little time for fishing at Grove Mills ..." [The booklet had contained a reference to fishing on its first page]

"At the end of the War, in 1919, 'Lyxhayr Manufacturers Ltd.' became 'Mitcham Fibre Mills Ltd.' and the freehold of their premises was purchased. Coinciding with this change came further expansion and the introduction of new products.

"One of these was the extraction of coir fibre from coconut husks. Huge piles of husks were treated in specially constructed soaking tanks and then passed to crushing and extractor machines which produced, among other things, fibes for the brush trade and cheaper grades of bedding. This section of the business continued until 1926 by which time the cheaper imported fibres made the Mitcham variety uneconomic.

"Mr. Dickinson retired in 1932 because of illness and Mr. Hedger took over the management. This particular year also saw all-round improvements in Lyxhayr manufacture, expecially in fixing the curl by more modern plant. In 1932 also, the use of one of the waterwheels was discontinued in favour of electric motors. By now the list of products being made included curled hair and fibre mixtures and also better qualities of curled hair. The demand for all these products rose from year to year despite the general slump in trade in the 'thirties and went on doing so up to 1939.

"When war came again Lyxhayr in particular soon went on service, the entire output being used for hospital bedding and mattresses in hospital ships and troop transports.

"In the Far Eastern War Lyxhayr solved quite a pressing problem. Few materials needed in this campaign could withstand the ravages of the tropical climate and insect attack without special 'Tropic-proofing'. The Ministry of Supply tested Lyxhayr under actual jungle conditions, confirmed that it was resistant to attack by insects, fungi etc., as well as rot-proof, and specified Lyxhayr as a material for upholstery in fighting vehicles which could be used without special 'Tropic-proofing' treatment.

"In November 1940 Grove Mills received a direct bomb hit which knocked a corner off one of the principal buildings erected only in 1938 and blasted many tons of debris into the tail race of the water mill. Army pioneers cleared all this in a week and the wheel itself ran as well as ever. Deliveries were not held up and it was a proud boast of the staff at Grove Mills that they managed to meet all demands in spite of the many handicaps imposed by war.

"After the war the tremendous demand for furniture and bedding fillings kept Grove Mills at full stretch month after month not only on Lyxhayr but also on the other products of the company. Not even the winter of 1947 was allowed to reduce the scale of activity very greatly.

"Many of our manufacturing friends will remember the great power shut down during the freeze-up in that year. No factories were allowed electric current for machines or lighting, which meant suspending operations in almost every case. At Grove Mills, however, the water wheel kept going all the time, and so enabled supplies of fillings to be kept up to firms still able to make upholstery by hand. The demand was, in fact, so brisk as to necessitate overtime working. The difficulty at Grove Mills was that the regulations precluded the use of electric power for lighting the factory. A telegram to the Ministry of Fuel and Power elicited the reply "Permission Granted" and so Grove Mills 'still kept going when the rest had stopped'.

"About this time the sound of the water wheel was recorded by Ludwig Koch for inclusion in a B.B.C. Third Programme broadcast of pleasant sounds.

"In 1948 further expansion at Grove Mills made necessary the formation of another company 'Mitcham Hair and Fibre Mills Ltd.' with Mr. Harold T. Turnbull as Chairman and Mr. E. B. Hedger as Managing Director.

"So it has gone on; each year has seen a growth in the business, extensions to the works, new machinery, more workers. Even today we have the builders in adding to our facilities and outbuildings to serve the needs of the bedding and furnishing industries.

"Between 1903 and 1953 Mitcham itself has changed enormously. The once tiny village surrounded by gardens and farms has become the largest industrial town in Surrey. Yet even today Grove Mills itself is still a pleasant spot with part of the adjoining land preserved by the National Trust and much of the remainder set out as playing fields.

"This modest story of the fifty years development of Grove Mills thus comes to an end, but it is not the end of this company's story. No doubt it will go on increasing its usefulness to industry. Perhaps Lyxhayr and the other fillings made at Grove Mills will be used in the future more for helicopters and jet-propelled airliners than for motor cars and lorries. But it seems very probable that Mitcham Hair and Fibre Mills will still be going strong in another fifty years from now."

------------

(The products listed on the back of the booklet were:

"Lyxhayr, Curled M.M.Fibre, Curlifill, Curled Hair and Fibre Mixtures and Curled Hair." E.N.M.)

*The Grove Mill in the mid-1960s (ENM)*
*At this time water from the Wandle was still flowing beneath the building.*

# APPENDIX II

## The Fire at Lyxhayr Ltd, Grove Mill, Mitcham 1907

Notes supplied by Mr E B Hedger on the members of the Mitcham Fire Brigade and others to be seen standing outside the gutted Grove Mill in the photograph reproduced opposite (reading from left to right):

| | |
|---|---|
| "Jack Schneider | Local turncock for the Metropolitan Water Board. Lived in Clarendon Grove. |
| Charlie Jordan | Employed by John S. Deed & Sons. Lived in one of the old timber 'Blue House'" cottages by the 'Ravensbury Arms' on Mitcham Common. |
| Herbert Sayers | Brother of Charles Sayers, founder of Charles Sayers & Son, the Mitcham builders. Herbert, I believe, was employed by Whiteheads the builders of Clapham. He lived in Edmund Road. |
| Walter Tapping | Lived in Benedict Road. I think he worked for Parsons. Later he was employed by the Council on the roads adjacent to the Fire Station, and was a part-time fireman. |
| Fred Harris | A well-known local sportsman and caddymaster at the Princes Golf Club on the Common. Lived in Edmund Road. |
| Jack Thomson | His father kept cows which grazed on the Common. Lived close to the 'Windmill'. His father used to take the milk round in two large milk pails suspended from a yoke across his shoulders. I remember seeing Jack helping his father, but cannot say whether he had any other occupation. |
| Walter Jordan | Then a sub-officer. Later to become Station Officer. At that time caretaker of St. Marks (Upper Mitcham) School. In later life worked for Thomas Parsons. |
| Mick Jordan | Worked for Lancaster. Lived in Church Place (Bull Yard). |
| George Chester | Worked for A. & C. Jenner |

| | |
|---|---|
| Charlie Skillern | Worked for livery stables adjoining the 'King's Head.' They provided the two horses to pull the steam fire engine in use at that time. Skillern drove them. Lived in one of the cottages adjoining the Council's depot in Church Road. At that time it was Guyatt's gravel pit. |
| John Smith | Foreman for Lyxhayr Ltd. Lived at 479 London Road. |
| W. A. Dickinson | Managing Director, Lyxhayr Ltd. |
| Mr. Seager | Lived in 475/477 London Road. He had a very small part of Crown Mill, in which he manufacturered or factored furniture polish. |
| Alfred Jenner | Of A. C. Jenner, the engineers. Also Superintendant of the Mitcham Fire Brigade. |
| Mr. Holmes | The chemist who first put on the market the patent horsehair. Mr. Dickinson and Mr. Holmes are both mentioned in my booklet *Fifty Years at Grove Mills, Mitcham* |
| The boy | Alfred Jenner's son." |

# APPENDIX III

## NOTE OF THE MAIN POINTS MADE AT A PUBLIC MEETING HELD ON 10 JANUARY 1996, CONCERNING THE WANDLE POLLUTION INCIDENT

At the meeting the National Rivers Authority was represented by Rachael Pennell, and Thames Water was represented by Helen Newman and by Jim Stacey (Manager at Beddington Works). This paper is a summary of the main points which emerged in the meeting.

1. THE WORKS AND THE WANDLE

The Beddington Works has a 3 hour storm water capacity. This capacity is provided so that the works can cope with short periods of very high rainfall. In "normal" conditions this capacity can be used to hold back contaminated liquids from entering the River Wandle.

The Wandle is especially vulnerable to pollution as 95% of the volume of the Wandle is made up of sewage effluent from the works, and there is therefore very little dilution effect possible. This is not the case with most rivers and most sewage works, where dilution occurs to a far greater extent.

2. THE STANDARDS

The current discharge consent standard consists of two parameters. Firstly ammoniacal nitrogen (to be not more that 25 milligrams per litre), and secondly biological oxygen demand (to be not more that 12 milligrams per litre). The ammoniacal nitrogen standard would be enough to kill the fish in the river. There is a "voluntary standard" agreed between the NRA and TW of between 5 and 10 milligrams per litre for ammoniacal nitrogen.

The 95 percentile standard means that 95% of samples taken should comply with the requirements laid down in the discharge consent given by the NRA. There is no purity standard at all for the other 5% of the samples. Compliance is measured using spot samples on a weekly basis, per year. Five sample failures are therefore permitted in any one year.

The consent given to TW therefore offers no guarantee that fish can survive in the Wandle, as periodic pollution will not contravene the consent.

The NRA confirmed that the 95% standard was laid down by statute, and not by common practice.

The water quality standard referred to in the Catchment Management Plan is rather academic, as this referred to a river quality objective for the Wandle of RE4 (suitable for coarse fish populations).

3. THE INCIDENT

TW were unable to explain why fish were dying in the river before the ammonium levels had risen. TW took the view that the incident occurred in Sunday 22 October. The NRA were trying to find out why fish were dying before that date.

The NRA were surprised that there had been no automatic alarm system operating at Beddington to detect ammonium. TW had also failed to inform the Trade Effluent Officer.

The lack of notification given to the riparian landowners meant that possible closing off of sections of the river, to exclude polluted water, could not be implemented. Closing off sections of the river might have allowed some fish to survive, for example in the various arms of the river at Morden Hall Park.

4. SINCE THE INCIDENT

TW had installed a toxicity meter at the intake to the works, which should detect any similar threat to the digesters in the sewage treatment works. This was new technology, and was not proven. Its installation at Beddington is on trial.

Ammonium monitoring of the effluent had been improved, and was now on a continuous monitoring basis. An alarm system had been installed linked to the ammonium monitor, and this would alert the control room of any high readings. The continuous monitoring of ammonium at Beddington was one of only a few known examples of this practice in the country.

The internal communications system, which had not worked during the incident, had been improved, and staff training had been given.

Monitoring would in future be carried out by TW, and they indicated that the results would be provided to all interested parties, if requested. This ought to include the NRA. Results would be available for past periods of time.

There was criticism that the NRA ought to do the monitoring themselves, rather than to rely on a potential culprit for the results of monitoring.

## 5. LIMITATIONS OF IMPROVEMENTS

Untreated or polluted effluent can only be held back from the river for a limited period, and this limitation was governed by the storage capacity on the site. .

TW were asked to consider increasing the storage capacity on the Beddington site, so as to increase the chances of being able to prevent pollutants from entering the sewage works or the river. They indicated that it was not worth while doing this in view of the cost and the low risk of a similar pollution incident. This did not sit well with their ready admission that a similar pollution incident could occur at any time. TW confirmed that it was for the NRA to "give guidance" on the storage capacity which should be provided.

The measurement of biological oxygen demand involved a 5 day test, and it could not therefore be done on a continuous basis. The point was put to TW that continuous monitoring was possible for a number of different parameters.

## 6. CONSULTATION AND INVESTMENT

Consultation forums were in place in some areas, to allow TW to bring in the local people to a discussion as to how their investment programme should be directed. There was no such forum in this area.

Phil Ryder

Wandle Heritage Ltd.

(Reproduced by permission)

*'The Wandle, Mitcham' – early 20th-century postcard of Mitcham Bridge*

*Mitcham Bridge, London Road, looking south towards Bishopsford Road*
Mitcham News and Mercury, *Summer 1971*

# NOTES AND REFERENCES

## Abbreviations Used

| | |
|---|---|
| Braithwaite | Braithwaite F, 'On the Rise and Fall of the River Wandle; its Springs, Tributaries and Pollution', *Proceedings of the Institution of Civil Engineers 20* (1861) |
| CLSL | Croydon Local Studies Library |
| Edwards | Edwards J, *Companion from London to Brighthelmston* (1801) |
| Francis | Francis T, 'Old Mitcham' (Notes on a collection of Lantern Slides) (MLSC) |
| Hedger | E B Hedger, former managing director of Mitcham Hair and Fibre Mills Ltd, interviewed in 1967 |
| Hoare | MLSC. Sale Particulars of the Estate of the late Henry Hoare. (Copies also in Sutton and Croydon local studies collections) |
| Malcolm | Malcolm J, *A Compendium of Modern Husbandry of Surrey I* (1805) |
| M & B | Manning O and Bray W, *The History and Antiquities of the County of Surrey* |
| MC | Copies of Mitcham Census Returns (MLSC) |
| MLSC | London Borough of Merton Local Studies Centre |
| MPR | Mitcham Poor Rate Books, (SHC) |
| MLT | Mitcham Land Tax Records, (SHC) |
| MoLT | Morden Land Tax records (SHC) |
| MoTS | Morden Tithe Commutation Survey (SHC). See also<br>*Morden in 1838: The Tithe Apportionment Map*, Merton Historical Society Local History Notes 13 (1998) |
| MTS | Mitcham Tithe Commutation Survey Register 1846 & Map 1847 (MLSC). See also<br>*Mitcham in 1846: The Tithe Apportionment Map*, Merton Historical Society Local History Notes 22 (2002) |
| Rice | Rice R Garraway, 'On the Parish Registers of Ss Peter and Paul, Mitcham', in *The Reliquary* (1877) (Copy in MLSC) |
| SHC | Surrey History Centre |
| *VCH* | *Victoria County History of Surrey* |

## MITCHAM BRIDGE

1 This hypothesis is explored more fully in the chapter on Wickford in Volume 4 in the Mitcham Histories Series *Lower Mitcham* (2003) 135-6

2 Montague E N *The Archaeology of Mitcham* (1991) 14-22

Many of the burials may, in fact, have been of the indigenous Romano-British people

3 CLSL William Marr's map of 1685. 'Mitcham Bridge' is clearly marked. (Map believed to have been transferred to SHC)

4 SHC Mitcham Vestry Minutes

5 M & B III (1814) Appendix xxvii.

6 Edwards Pt II 18

## THE WANDLE FISHERY

1 Gough's translation (Camden wrote in Latin)

Although it has often been asserted that Izaak Walton, that doyen of anglers, mentioned the Wandle in *The Compleat Angler* this is not so, and it is only in notes to two of the later editions of his work that references to the river can be found. (Note by Judith Goodman, pers. com., 18 January 1996)

2 Hobson J, *Book of the Wandle* (1924) 93/4

3 MLSC Revd Herbert Randolph's notebook. See also

*Parishioners of Mitcham 1837/38: The Revd Herbert Randolph's Notebook*, Merton Historical Society Local History Notes 20 (2002) 6

4 Davy H, *Salmonia; or Days of Dry Fly Fishing* (edition of 1869) 50, 52

5 Torre C, *Small Talk at Wreyland* (1970) 30

S P Torre is listed in Green's *South London Directory* (1869) 124 as resident at Brookfields Cottage, Wandle Grove.

6 Francis 28

7 Braithwaite 199 -

8 Kelly's *Directory* 1895

9 E B Hedger assured me in an interview in 1967 that Bourne kept his trays of fry in an old wooden building upstream in the Watermeads, and not in the derelict snuff mill in Morden meadow as stated by Tom Francis in his lecture notes and in the captions to several photographs in Mitcham Library.

10 E B Hedger confirmed Bourne's date of leaving with an old lady who once lived at No. 479.

11 SHC Agreement between the Corporation of Croydon and Capt H F Bidder and others as to the Wandle Fisheries.

12 Francis 29

13 Lt Col Harold F Bidder DSO, MA, FSA, is remembered for his excavation of the 'Anglo-Saxon' cemetery at Mitcham, and his work on the site of Merton Priory. He was first President of Merton and Morden Historical Society (now the Merton Historical Society).

14 In 1922 William Simpson sold his house, Park Place, Commonside West, to the *News of the World*, who converted the surrounding land into a sports ground, and used the building as a club house. It is now (2004) occupied as a restaurant.

15 See Appendix III

## THE WATERMEADS AND HAPPY VALLEY

### Acquisition by the National Trust

1 *Properties of the National Trust* (1973) 143

2 Wimbledon Society's Museum. *Report of the Wandle Open Spaces Committee* 1914

3 Upcott J, 'Octavia Never Looked Sideways' in *National Trust Newsletter* No. 8 June 1970, 6

4 Inscribed "This seat is placed on land part of which was given in memory of Miranda Hill by some of her grateful and affectionate pupils. Born January lst 1836, died May 31st 1910."

5 Clark E F, *George Parker Bidder. The Calculating Boy* (1983) 62

There may have been further purchases after the passing of the Carew Estate Act 1857

6 To minimise disturbance to wild life and limit vandalism the Trust's policy (2004) is to limit access, but keys are obtainable on loan, from the Estate Manager at Morden Hall Park.

7 MoLT

### The Early History of the Watermeads

8 M & B II (1809) 499, quoting Claus. 35 Edw. III m.3, dors.

See also *Calendar of Close Rolls Edw. III, XI* (1908) 302

**The Mill Sites**

9 Malcolm 6

**The 'Jack' Pond**

10 Francis 39

**Inter-War Perspectives**

11 Francis 132

12 Francis 29-31

**Current Management Policy**

13 Outlined by Rachel Thomkins, Manager of the National Trust's Wandle Properties, in a conversation with the writer in January 2004

## THE MILL COTTAGES (Nos. 475-479 London Road)

1 MPR

2 There is no entry in the 1851 census records which can be related to this house.

3 They are included in the 33rd List of Buildings of Special Architectural or Historic Interest as at 2nd September 1988, compiled by the Secretary of State for the Environment under the Town and Contry Planning Act 1971 with the comment:

> "TQ 26 NE London Road, Mitcham (East side)
>
> Serial No. 4/87. Nos. 475 to 479 (odd) (Mill Cottages)
>
> Date first listed: 11. 10. '74. Grade II."

4 Information from E B Hedger in 1967.

## THE MILLS BY MITCHAM BRIDGE

**Early History**

1 Morris J, *Domesday Book: Surrey* (1975) 21 1 and 2

2 British Library. MS Add. 6040 f1 No. 20
(Transcription by John Blair supplied in personal communication).

3 *VCH* IV (1912) 233 quoting Anct.D. (National Archives/PRO) A 9189

4 M & B II (1809) 499, quoting Claus. 35 Edw. III h.3. dors. See also *Calendar of Close Rolls, Edward III XI* (1908) 302

5 *VCH* IV (1912) 233 quoting Inq. a.g.d. 395, no.28

6 *VCH* IV (1912) 233

7 Hopkins P, 'Morden Hall before Morden Hall' in *Merton Historical Society Bulletin* 143 (2003) 6

8 SHC 212/73/1

9 Will dated 1. 1. 1529/30, proved 23. 2. 1529/30

Ref. Archdeaconry of Surrey, Mychell Register, LMA: DW/PA/7/3 fol. 125r & 129v WSFHS MW3:73

10 *VCH* IV (1912) 233, quoting *Valor Eccl.* (Rec. Com), ii, 48

11 Heales A, *The Records of Merton Priory* (1898) p.cxxv.

Ministers Accounts, Co. Surrey, 29-30 Henry VIII, No.115, Mem. 7

12 MTS

13 SHC 599/219 a-b

14 SHC Mitcham Baptismal Registers. Baptism of Thomas Smythe's natural son Edward

15 Rice R G, 'On the Parish Registers of Ss. Peter and Paul, Mitcham' *The Reliquary* (1877) 22/3 Note 49

16 London County Council *Court Minutes of the Surrey and Kent Sewer Commissioners* (1909) 120

17 Rice R G, 'On the Parish Registers of Ss. Peter and Paul, Mitcham' *The Reliquary* (1877) 141 Note 28. Will dated 6 Jan. 1575/6 SHC 212/73/22

18 SHC 77/4/1

19 In 1593 he had been appointed High Collector of the Lay Subsidy in the Hundred of Wallington.

20 Guiseppi H S, 'The River Wandle in 1610' in *Surrey Archaeological Collections* 21 (1908) 170-191

SHC 212/113/18: During a survey of the manor of Reigate in 1623 it was noted that as a freeholder

"George Smyth, gent., holdeth also of this Mannor one Tenement and water Milne and 30 acres of marsh ground lyinge at Mitcham for which he payeth the yearly Rent of xxs."

21 SHC 212/113/18a

22 *VCH* IV (1912) 232, quoting Chan. Proc. Hh, 17 Eliz. no.3; also Pat.30 Eliz. pt. vi, m.14

23 Correspondence in September 1940 between the steward of the manor of Reigate and E B Hedger.

**Copper Milling (1698-c.1748)**

1 SHC 3537/1/21 p.50 entry 63

2 SHC 3537/1/23 p.23

3 SHC 303/21/4/4

4 Day J and Tylecote R F (editors), *The Industrial Revolution in Metals* (1991), and Michael Wilks (pers. comm. 20 Jan. '95)

5 Milward R, *Wimbledon in the Time of the Civil War* (1976) 75

6 MLSC Tom Francis Scrapbook. Undated cutting from Mitcham Advertiser: Letter from G A Hannaford, 11 Raleigh Gardens, Mitcham.

7 SHC 145/26

At a court baron of the manor of Reigate held in June 1726 the death was announced of widow Smith, seized of a water mill at Mitcham and messuage. " - Miers, gent.", was named as her heir.

(This would have been the "Sussanah Smyth" of Mitcham who in her will dated 13 Feb. 1724, probate 30 July 1725, left her Mitcham estate to "her kinsman" William Myers of King Street, London. Prob 11 604 162.)

At another court baron of the same manor, held in July 1742, William Myers Esq. was announced as having held of the manor as a freehold tenant a watermill and 30 acres of marsh ground at a yearly rental of 20s. The property passed to his son.

(In his will dated 13 Oct 1739 proved at London 29 July 1742, William Myers, after various small bequests, left to his son William "all real estate copyhold as well as freehold by virtue of Will or settlement of Sussana Smith late of Mitcham". Prob 11 719 226)

8 SHC 303/21/4/1

**The Flour Mills (1765-1795)**

1 SHC 303/21/4/2

2 MPR

3 SHC 303/21/4/3

4 Montague E, *Lower Mitcham* (2003) 62-5

5 Montague E, *The Cricket Green* (2001) 76

6 SHC 303/21/4/2 7 August 1765 and 303/21/4/3 8 August 1765

7 SHC 303/21/4/4

8 Montague E, *Lower Mitcham* (2003) 68

9 MPR

In 1768, for instance, John Chesterman was occupying a house and mill with a combined rateable value of £93.

10 SHC Counterpart of lease dated 16 September 1772, 303/21/4/5

11 MLT and

Montague E, *Pollards Hill, Commonside East and Lonesome* (2002) 67

12 MS 8674/115 p.173, and National Archives 11/1113 q 70, quoted by Peter McGow in pers. comm. 5. 9. '01

13 Berry W, *Pedigrees of Surrey* (1837) 110.

Valentine A, *The British Establishment* I (1970) 363 - 4 has the following note on another, presumably related, Richard Glover (1712 - 85):

"Of Exchange Alley, London: son of Richard Glover (Hamburg merchant of London). He entered his father's business c.1728 and also wrote and published verse. In 1737 he married Hannah Nunn, "a lady of property", but in 1756 he divorced her for the usual reason. His opposition to Sir Robert Walpole won him in 1744 a legacy of £500 from the Duchess of Marlborough. He was supported for election to Parliament by Bubb Doddington, who largely controlled the seat he secured (Weymouth and Melcombe Regis). As a merchant-banker he secured a share in government loans and several times addressed the House on behalf of merchant interests. Though a verbose speaker, some thought he had boldness and energy, and he was "a popular leader at elections". He was listed as a Tory in 1761. He supported Bute but opposed the cider tax in 1763, and was thereafter classed as "doubtful" in the various lists compiled by both parties of members of the House ... He wrote and collected verse and plays and also acted, on occasions at the Drury Lane Theatre."

14 Several members of the Glover family are commemorated by ledger stones in the paving of the south aisle of Mitcham parish church, but these are now covered by a raised floor:

Sarah Glover, d.1703 daughter of Gabriel and Bridget Glover

Gabriel Glover, d.1706 son of Gabriel and Bridget Glover

Bridget Glover, d.1709 aged 36, wife of Gabriel Glover Esq.

Mary Glover, d.1717 aged 18, daughter of Gabriel and Bridget

Gabriel Glover, d.1723 aged 61, and

Ann Glover, d.1751 aged 50, daughter of Gabriel and Bridget.

15 She died at Mitcham, but is buried at Warlingham.

Berry, op. cit..

16 MLT:

Two mills: Proprietor, Samuel Fry, occupiers Richard Glover and John Chesterman.

17 Guildhall Library, Sun Fire Insurance Policy 505278 1/6/85

18 SHC Mitcham vestry minutes, Vol. 2 1763-1793.

19 SHC (Ex. Guildford Muniment Room) 51/10/7 (1) - (18).

Will and Probate of John Chesterman 31 Jan. 1784. Proved 19 Feb. 1784.

Another John Chesterman, a miller and maltster, and presumably his son, is referred to after the death of Chesterman in 1784. The collection of family papers also includes doctors' bills for attending to "Debbic" Chesterman.

20 PRO 11/1113 q 70 Quoted by McGow

21 Edwards II 18:

"About half a furlong to the left" (i.e. of the main road) "is Mitcham corn-mill. It was burnt down in the year 1788; and it is now rebuilding. It is the property of W. Fry Esq., and was lately occupied by Samuel Chesterman".

22 Malcolm J, I (1805) 7

**The Snuff Mills (1772 - 1845)**

1 MLSC Notes by Tom Francis to Miss Farewell Jones, dated 1932. He referred to the mill as "Caleb Raleigh's mill" as though this was the name by which it had been generally known in his youth in the latter part of the 19th century.

2 SHC 303/21/4/5

3 Edwards II 18

4 Guildhall Library, Royal Exchance Fire Insurance Policy No. 244523 8 March 1809

5 MoLT

6 Guildhall Library, Royal Exchange Fire Insurance Policy No. 244523. It was noted that there was no steam engine in this mill.

7 MLSC Local history collection

8 MLSC Local history collection

Unfortunately details of the lot which included the mills are missing from the MLSC collection. (Copies of the sale particulars are also in Sutton and Croydon local studies collections)

9 MLSC MSS account of the 'Perambulation of the Boundary Line of the Parish of Mitcham ... 16th May 1833"

(Book last seen when in the Merton Chief Executive's Department. Present whereabouts now unknown)

10 SHC 'Book of Reference' dated 29 November 1834. Listing "Names of Owners etc. of Property taken under authority of Act of Parliament for the extraction of water from the Wandle at Waddon Mills."

11 MoTS (Dated 5 August 1837):

Mrs Spencer (late Fry) - landowner; Richard Glover - occupier:

Ref: 303A Garden

304 Paddock

305 Paddock and snuff mill

Hopkins P, *Morden in 1838*, Merton Historical Society Local History Notes 13 (1998)

12 Surrey Archaelogical Society Library Mitcham folder

13 Hopkins P & Turner S, *Mitcham in 1838*, Merton Historical Society Local History Notes 21 (2002)

14 Robson's *Commercial Directory* 1839:

"Richard Glover, Lower Mitcham. Snuff and Tobacco Merchant."

Pigot and Co.'s *Directory* 1839 – ditto,

*Post Office Directory* 1845:

"Glover, Richard, snuff grinder, Lower Mitcham." and

The *Post Office Directory* of 1845, which is the last to list Richard Glover as a snuff grinder.

15 Braithwaite 200

16 Francis

17 Hillier J, *Old Surrey Water-Mills* (1951) 178/9

Unfortunately, as a source of historical fact, Hillier is not entirely reliable.

18 MC 1841

19 MTS:

| | | |
|---|---|---|
| 1292 | Meadow | ) Glover, Richard |
| 1289 | House, gardens and buildings) | ) " |
| 1291 | Kiln House, yard and buildings | ) Unoccupied |
| 1294 | Snuff mills | ) " |

Hopkins P, *Mitcham in 1846* Merton Historical Society Local History Notes 22 (2002)

**The Paper Mill**

1 MLSC Hoare

2 Crocker A, 'Watermarks in Surrey Hand-made Paper' in *Surrey History* III No.1, (1984/5), 7

3 Information from Alan Crocker, in a personal communication, quoting SHC 5/10/79 and 10/11/19, Shorter A H, 'Paper Mills and paper makers in England' (1957) and 'Paper Making in the British Isles' (1971) 236.

4 Guildhall Library, Sun Fire Insurance Policy No. 890986

5 MLSC ? MS. account by Edwin Chart of Beating of the Bounds of Mitcham in 1833.

6 SHC 'Book of Reference' dated 29th November 1834

7 MoTS

**The Surrey Iron Railway**

1 Hillier J, *Old Surrey Water-Mills* (1951) 177 and

Francis 32

Whether Tom Francis knew this as a fact, or was relying on Hillier, is not clear.

2 This was the view expressed to the writer by E B Hedger.

**John Glover, Flour Miller (1833 - 1855)**

1 MLSC Hoare

2 SHC Book of Reference 1834

3 Robson's *Commercial Directory* 1839: "John Glover, Lower Mitcham, Miller"

and

Pigot's *Directory of Surrey* 1839.

4 MC 1841 and 1851.

5 MTS:

Richard Spencer - landowner; John Glover - occupier:

1290 House, garden & buildings

1293 Garden

1295 Flour Mills

6 Braithwaite 200

7 MLSC Festival Brochure of 1951, produced by Mitcham Borough Council. A photograph of the mill wheel is captioned "Potential 90 h.p. Actual 25 h.p.".

**The Crown and Grove Mills (1850 - 1900) Felt and Flour**

1 MTS

2 MC 1841 and 1851

3 Hillier J, *Old Surrey Water-Mills* (1951) 178/9

Unfortunately, as a source of historical facts, Hillier is not entirely reliable.

4 Braithwaite 200

5 *Post Office Directory* 1862. "Whitehead & Co., Felt Manufacturers"

6 Information from E B Hedger [He was grandson of Benjamin Slater, lavender grower, whose 'Memories of Old Mitcham' were published in *Old Mitcham* (1923), general editor H F Bidder.]

Hedger pointed out that in his lecture notes (MLSC) Tom Francis is incorrect on page 31 when he implies that this waterwheel, portrayed in one of his slides, belonged to the Grove flour mill.

7 Short M, *Windmills in Lambeth* (1971) 60.

8 *Post Office Directories*, 1845 and 1851.

9 Kelly's *Directory* 1890;

"Ashby, Joseph and Sons, millers (water), Wandlemills, Lower Mitcham"

Kelly's *Directory* 1899:

"Ashby, Joshua and Sons, millers (water), Wandle Mills, Sutton Road,

Lower Mitcham.

(Not in 1903 Directory)

10 Hedger E B, *50 Years at Grove Mills, Mitcham. The Story of Lyxhayr and Service to the Bedding and Upholstery Trades by Mitcham Hair and Fibre Mills Ltd.* (1953).

(Copy donated to Mitcham Library in 1967, but stated to have been 'lost' on enquiry in 1993). For extracts, see Appendix I)

**Mitcham Hair and Fibre Mills (1903–1955)**

1 Higgs T, *300 Years of Mitcham Cricket* (1985) 14 and

Hitchen W E *Surrey at the Opening of the Twentieth Century* (1906) 170:

"William Wright Thompson J.P. of Mitcham, born South Africa 1846. Director of R.R.Whitehead Brothers Ltd. of Greenfield, Yorkshire and Mitcham. Late member of Surrey County Council for Carshalton. One of the first members of the Board of Conservators, Mitcham Common; on the Committee of Surrey County Cricket Club; Captain and Hon. Sec. of Mitcham Cricket Club; Founder and first Treasurer of Mitcham Freemasons' Lodge."

In the 1870s Thompson was living at Tamworth Lodge, Commonside East.

2 The 1910 Ordnance Survey map shows the mill as 'disused'.

Kelly's *Directory* for 1905 contains the last reference to Whiteheads:

> "Whitehead R. R. and Bros. Ltd. Wandle Felt Works, Sutton Road, Lower Mitcham."

The 1905 Kelly's also lists Lyxhayr Ltd., (W A Dickinson, sec.), horsehair substitute manufacturers (patent), Grove Mills.

3 This, at least, is what E B Hedger had been told as a lad. He joined Lyxhayr after Seager had left the Crown Mill, and one wonders if 'furniture polish' was what the workmen at the fibre mills told him Seager had been making when, in fact, it was Dutch gin. There is no corroborative evidence from contemporary directories.

4 The occupier of No. 475. (Henry Smith) in a conversation in 1994.

5 MLSC Various old post cards survive showing the mill before and after the fire.

6 Hedger E B *op cit*

7 Hillier J, *Old Surrey Water Mills* (1951) 178/9

8 Hedger E B *op cit*

## 'WANDLE GROVE' OR 'WANDLE HOUSE', AND THE BROOKFIELDS ESTATE

1 33rd List, dated 2nd September 1988, compiled under the Town and Country Planning Act 1971, section 54;

TQ 25 NE. Serial number 4/116. First listed 16. 1. 54. Grade II.

"Detached house now offices. Circa 1795. Attributed to Robert Mylne, Brown brick, tuck pointed. Slate mansard roof to parapet. 2 storeys. Western elevation of 3 windows wide. Square gauged headed windows, sashes, glazing bars. Ground floor windows in semi-circular headed reveals. Stucco band between storeys. Cornice above first floor. Parapet with panels on balustrading. South facade with 2 storey segmental bay window. East return to road also of architectural interest. Present entrance through adjoining office block of 1963, which is not of special interest".

The house was also listed in *Antiquities of Surrey* (1965) with comment: "No. 1888/ No.10 (Wandle House) Riverside Drive. (c.1780)".

2 Nairn I and Pevsner N, *Buildings of Surrey* (1971). 56 and 372.

3 SHC 303/21/4/4

4 MLT

It was suggested in a local paper in the 1960s that Lady Hamilton had slept at 'Wandle Grove'. The house was certainly standing during her lifetime, but without corroborative evidence, the story has to be treated as journalistic speculation.

5 Edwards.

Significantly, 'Wandle Grove' receives no mention in the text, which from its general content seems to have been compiled around 1789. Edward's map, however, dated c. 1801 indicates a house on the site of 'Wandle Grove', approached by a drive.

6 Greenwood, C & J, *Surrey Described* (1823) 294.

7 MLSC Hoare

8 They were recorded in the census return in 1841, William Wilson being described as of 'independent means'.

9 Wilson, Mary (Editor, Jennifer Simpson) *A European Journal – Two Sisters Abroad in 1847* (1987) 12-14

10 *Alumni Oxiensus*, *Alumni Cantabrigensus*, and Crockford's *Clerical Directory* (1865), also

MLSC Revd Herbert Randolph's Notebook published as *Parishioners of Mitcham 1837/38: The Revd Herbert Randolph's Notebook*, Merton Historical Society Local History Notes 20 (2002)

11 *VCH* IV (1912) 234.

12 MTS:

| Reference | 1298 House, garden and building | ) | |
|---|---|---|---|
| | 1299 Orchard | ) | |
| | 1300 Shrubbery | ) | 11 acres 1r.11p |
| | 1301 Field Meadow | ) | |
| | 1302 Lodge Meadow. | ) | |

13 Henry Hopkins' stay at 'Wandle Grove' could have been only of short duration, for he was not mentioned in the local directory for 1845, and must have moved away by 1848, when William Wilson was said to be in residence (See reference 11).

14 MC 1851.

15 *Post Office Directory* entry for Mitcham, 1851.

16 Green's *South London Directory* 1869.

17 SHC (Ex Guildford Muniment Room) 303/21/4/7/

A detailed inventory of fixtures and fittings survives.

18 *Kelly's Directory*, 1882.

19 Mr Daniels, former groundsman to Hovis Ltd, interviewed in 1967.

20 Hedger

21 *Mitcham News* 11 March 1960.

22 *Mitcham News and Mercury* 29 April 1966.

23 Information kindly supplied by A H Armstrong, Director of Coppas International (UK) Ltd, in December 1979.

By May 1985 Coppas International had moved away, and Wandle House was vacant.

## THE SURREY BREWERY

1 Francis p.89. No. 185.

2 MLSC Document of release in local history collection L2(347.2).

3 Edwards, Pt. II, 18

4 MLSC Map of Henry Hoare's estate, dated 1812. The site of the brewery is marked "The Exors. of the Late Mr. Hughes"

5 MS 8674/105 p. 144, quoted by Peter McGow in pers. comm., 5. 9. 2001

6 MS 8674/115 p.173 (McGow)

7 PROB 11/1012 q.405 (McGow)

8 MS 8674/124 p.9 (McGow)

9 PROB 11/1113 q 70 (McGow)

10 MS 8674/135 p.252 (McGow)

11 MS 8674/139 p.285 (McGow)

12 Hughes bequeathed all his leashold properties in Mitcham and Cheam to his wife Harriet. PROB 11/1430 q 589 (McGow)

13 MLSC Hoare

14 *The Times* 27 March 1817 (McGow)

15 Pigot's *Directory of Surrey* (1824/5)

16 *The London Gazette* 1 March 1817 (McGow)

17 MC 1841

18 *Post Office Directory* 1845 "Wilson, John, brewer, Globe Brewery, Lower Mitcham"

19 MTS

20 Shown as such on plan dated 1853, prepared for the private Bill presented to Parliament to enable the Wimbledon to Croydon railway to be built. SHC

21 Ordnance Survey map 1867

22 MLSC Mss. notes by John Lucas filed at LP 994 L2 (628.1) LUC, quoting *London Wells* (1913)

23 MC 1851

*'Wandle, Mitcham' – Postcard by Jenn*
*Crown Felt Mill on right.*
*Stream in bottom right hand corner is tail race of Crown Mill.*

*'Millstream, Mitcham' – Frith postcard*

# INDEX